Violent America:
The Movies
1946–1964

by Lawrence Alloway

The Museum of Modern Art, New York

Distributed by New York Graphic Society Ltd.

Greenwich, Connecticut

Published by The Museum of Modern Art, 1971
11 West 53 Street, New York, N.Y. 10019
Library of Congress Catalog Card Number
69-11452
Cloth Binding   ISBN 0-87070-623-3
Paperbound   ISBN 0-87070-622-5
Type set by Craftsman Type Inc., Dayton, Ohio
Printed and bound by Ray Freiman & Company
in the Netherlands

For Sylvia, anyway

Contents

The Lady from Shanghai, Columbia Pictures Corp.

Introduction

The origin of this book was a film series shown at The Museum of Modern Art from April 24 to June 6 1969, under the title *The American Action Movie: 1946–1964.* The title originally proposed, the one given this book, could not be used owing to the refusal of one of the film companies to lend prints to a series so entitled. The series began as a collaboration with Toby Mussman and Robert Smithson, and we conceived it as a survey of several genres of popular American movies, but this was too broad. Smithson, whose particular interest is science-fiction movies, withdrew when that genre was regretfully dropped from the series as the Museum scheduled a separate one on the subject; and Mussman moved to California. The series in its final form was my responsibility. Credits for all the movies in the series are given in an Appendix, along with excerpts from the program notes. Adrienne Mancia of the Department of Film, who initiated the project with Mussman, was a constant support in working in what is still a raw area for study.

The popular film is at once overfamiliar and understudied, which made me want to try to fill in a context of relevant ideas. Hence my interest in such topics as the pleasure of tragedy, which today is not very different from the appeal of violence; hence my curiosity about the concept of catharsis. Movies are dominated by conventions and can be grouped in cycles; that is the reason that so many movies had to be cited in the text (the first time a movie is mentioned its release date is given). In movies the actors are as stereotyped as, say, the young hero or the old warrior types in Renaissance portraiture. Situations are as recurrent in movies as the set themes of speeches in Seneca's plays, such as "the 'simple life' speech," "the 'haunted grove' speech," and "the 'king must be obeyed' speech," to quote E. F. Watling (see note 68). Thus my assumption that movies are a formulaic art is not a negative one. This essay is especially concerned with the transformations of meaning undergone by set figures and set situations, revealed by the forms of movie violence under the pressure of the contemporary world.

Though the book is a short one my acknowledgments go back some time. I want to thank three Talks producers on the Third Programme of the British Broadcasting Corporation for my first chance to discuss popular films: Leonie Cohn, D. S. Carne Ross, and George Macbeth. The dozen or so film reviews I did for them between 1955 and 1960 provide the basis of my approach to movies. Ian Cameron of *Movie,* Irving Kristol then of *Encounter,* and Sam Edwards when he was at *Arts,* were willing to publish an art critic's film criticism; I am grateful to them. My thanks for permission to cannibalize bits of these pieces, including parts of an article in *Vogue.* I am very grateful to Dr. Arthur C. Carr for his kindness in introducing me to the library of the Psychiatric Institute at Columbia University, to Steve Sally for making his stills collection available, to Robert Carter, former Director of Publications at the Museum, for his criticism and patience (which made the difference), and to Christie Kaiser for her editing of the manuscript.   L.A.

7

The Steel Helmet, Lippert Pictures.

Position Paper

Any discussion of popular movies, or indeed of film in general, must tackle the problem of realism. People like myself, who were born and brought up in Europe and came to the United States later, are possibly in a privileged position to answer the question, "How realistic are American movies?" My first visit to this country, after years of consuming Hollywood movies, answered the question positively. The United States is like its image in the movies, despite the conviction of most American and some foreign film critics that Hollywood's America is a false scene. Parker Tyler called it *The Hollywood Hallucination.*[1] Dissent about the iconicity (one-to-one correspondence of sign and referent) of the movies often takes the form of allowing that movies may have a surface realism, but that this conceals a historical falsity. This dualistic view oversimplifies the nature of cinematic realism. Discussing the role of indigenous places and things in American painting, Constance Rourke pointed out that "Posture, gesture, movement, bone structure, ranges of individual expression—these inevitably suggest underlying social ideas and emotions and motives in terms of typical form."[2] This perception of realism as a complex of physical details and implicit meanings is singularly applicable to a discussion of the movies. A definition of realism in the movies must allow for the connotative dimension of gesture and style as well as for the level of declarative statement.

If, as I believe, the movie camera has registered the topography and the sociology of the country with amazing fidelity, it is necessary to define "fidelity." A frequent example of American lack of realism has to do with the glamour of stars and with the domestic technology of homes in soap operas. The argument is that to audiences outside the industrialized and affluent United States, feminine enhancement and mechanized kitchens are fantasy material. If, instead of taking the glamour and the gadgets literally, we regard them as typical forms, the realistic basis of the movies can be affirmed even in this nest of artifice. In most of the world both the social and economic positions of women are improving; certainly most of the global audience for movies is benefiting from the domestic application of technology. A Hollywood kitchen may have more and newer appliances than the women in the audience have, but the kind and level of technology is not essentially different. Kitchen equipment has not changed fundamentally since the early 20th century; it has only been refined and elaborated. Hence, a supposed dream kitchen does correspond to the possessions of most of the audience; it is simultaneously more and the same.

To identify the realistic elements in movies, therefore, it is necessary to relate the imagery on the screen to the typical experiences of the large audience, which is after all a natural step in the discussion of a mass medium. In the 20th century more women can achieve beauty for longer periods of their lives than ever before, and they are accustomed to technological aids in domestic work. Most, if not all, of the machine-studded environment of movies and the typical dazzle of the stars can therefore be considered realistic as an index of the social experience of technical change.

It is necessary to decode the movies if we are to locate their realistic core. In fact all realist styles of art, literary or visual, are mediated by conventions, formal structures that lead from the outward display to the content. The 19th-century equation of realism with reform is also an obstacle in appreciating movies. It is naive to believe that the more stark a film is in style and the more underprivileged its characters, the more realistic it is. The tendency to link documentation with social protest ended as a vital impulse with, at the latest, *The Grapes of Wrath,* 1940. On the contrary, in movies realism is often to be identified with highly elaborate exposition. This area of the complex simulation of physical plausibility and of social reference has been called by Reuel Denney "the high cost of realism." Referring to the abundance of techniques available in the movie industry, Denney pointed out that "where audiences for Belasco productions once generated a need for craftsmanship because realism was the commodity they wanted, we now generate a need for realism because crafts and techniques stand wanting to be used."[3] The nature of the photographic image is, as will be argued later, irreducibly realistic.

The fantastic and the realistic are frequently expressed together. In Ian Fleming's *Thunderball,* one of the James Bond novels, the story line has to do with two nuclear bombs getting into the hands of a criminal group that plans to hold the world for ransom. Now this is a variant on the paranoid world-conspiracy theme of so many novels and films. Bond reflects gloomily that as weapons get smaller and more destructive such incidents are likely to increase. Soon "every little tin-pot nation would be making atomic bombs in their backyards . . . Apparently there was no secret now about the things. It had only been the prototypes that had been difficult."[4] The danger of such weapons and of radioactive material being stolen is a real one, carefully guarded against at military airfields, nuclear reactors, and laboratories. The archaic form of the conspiracy theme, therefore, echoing the Doctors Mabuse and Fu Manchu, does not exclude accurate and topical play with the risks of current weaponry (the point was preserved in the film version of the book in 1965).

Another mass art which compounds topical events with traditional plots and set figures is the comic strip. Daniel J. Leab proposed the term "cold war comics" for bellicose comic strips in newspapers for the period 1957–1963.[5] Strips such as *Terry, Captain Easy,* and *Dan Flagg,* are characterized by what Leab calls "a high public-affairs content" enforced by "naturalistic detail."[6] Cold-war comics are a revival and intensification of the strips of the 30s and early 40s, but given urgency by their attachment to new crises. Leab points out that the unnamed foreign powers Americans used to fight in peacetime are now specifically identified as Russian or Chinese Communists. The equivalent of cold-war comics in the movies can be found in slightly earlier movies, such as Samuel Fuller's *The Steel Helmet, Pickup on South Street,* and *Hell and High Water,* all made in the first half of the 50s. In *Pickup on South Street,* 1953, a New York pickpocket gets pushed into the world of "public affairs" when he accidentally lifts microfilm from a girl's purse. From the political indifference of a professional criminal he moves to a vengeful chase of women-killing commies. *Hell and High Water,* 1954, deals with an American-Chinese incident in the Arctic; this film has CinemaScope's first A-bomb explosion, and it names Communism explicitly as the new enemy, less than ten years after the end of World War II.

Connections between films often do not depend on the traditional definition of personal authorship, as can be seen by reference to two Korean War films by different directors, *The Steel Helmet,* 1951, and *One Minute to Zero,* 1952. In both the heroes are displayed in stances that earlier, more innocent phases of popular culture would have avoided. In Fuller's film an American sergeant shoots a prisoner of war, and in *One Minute to Zero,* directed by Tay Garnett, an American colonel orders the bombardment of a refugee column that he correctly suspects of being infiltrated by North Korean guerillas. In both cases the hero is placed in situations that cannot be resolved happily or sentimentally. It is not hard to see both episodes as part of a single response to the Korean War: "What are we doing here? Let's fight hard and get out." Both heroes are aggressive and laconic, with a zero-degree of tolerance, and they feel no need to justify their actions to others.

Fuller produced, wrote, and directed a film in which the violent act is brilliantly contextualized. Sergeant Zack, sole survivor of an illegal execution of prisoners by North Koreans, later shoots a North Korean officer after the man is contemptuous of the death of a South Korean child reluctantly adopted by the sergeant. The shooting is an unpremeditated act of high exasperation, the culmination of too much combat and fatigue. Underlying this causation is the fact that the Korean is a major, higher in rank than any American officer shown in the film. Zack is steadily scornful of his own lieutenant who is nervous and inept; thus, his contempt for officers reinforces his killer's instinct toward "gooks."

Shooting an enemy and shooting an officer are actions that support each other in *The Steel Helmet.* Something similar occurs in *Attack!,* 1956, in which Jack Palance plays a lieutenant as if he were a sergeant; his relation with his superior officers is entirely antagonistic. Probably owing to the success of John Wayne's Sergeant Stryker in *The Sands of Iwo Jima,* 1949, sergeants, who make the short-term decisions on the field close to the men, were a popular type at this time. In *One Minute to Zero,* the colonel, played by Robert Mitchum is, so to say, sergeantized. The colonel, though acting at the command level, has another power level to gripe about, that represented by the United Nations, which makes his decisions more complicated. The colonel is contemptuous of the U.N. presence in Korea, and his comments on the organization have a blunt, untheoretical belligerence. In *Attack!* there is a sequence in which the injured sergeant-as-lieutenant drags himself through a Nazi-occupied town to kill the American captain who had failed to give support to his platoon. The sergeant was regarded as the type of pragmatic efficiency. In both *The Steel Helmet* and in *Attack!* there is a savage skepticism about unqualified men in combat. An explicit working out of this theme is in *Men in War,* 1957, which is basically a dialogue between a sergeant with a killer instinct (which is always right) and an officer who reasons before shooting. The officer is not unsympathetic nor wrong, only less adapted than the sergeant to the Korean landscape. Their relationship begins as antagonistic and becomes symbiotic. The emphasis of these films is on survival and cooperation, a visual image of which is the shot in *The Steel Helmet* of Zack and a black medic sitting back to back to take snipers in the jungle trees.

War films of the 50s about Korea, as well as retrospective World War II subjects (these started four years after the end of the war), have attitudes in common. There is a warlike patriotism, a pragmatic willingness to kill when that is required by the situation, and a highly developed short-term skepticism about moral principles. These elements are not an avowed part of the American character, but a belief in the use of violence as an instrument is widespread. Both the Pentagon and its student critics, both radical blacks and the veterans of the wars before Vietnam, reveal a high tolerance of violence. It is present as part of the covert culture of the United States, though not a generally admitted characteristic.

The concept of covert culture, as developed by Bernard Bowron, Leo Marx, and Arnold Rose, is useful in the analysis of popular culture. Covert culture is neither the product of specific cultural subgroups nor is it the real but hidden values of a society. It can be defined as the "traits of culture rarely acknowledged,"[7] including those shady habits, archaic responses, and contradictory impulses that are sufficiently general to form patterns of related ideas and images. Part of the covert culture which is revealed by American popular art has to do with violence; there seems to be a greater interest in violence in the mass audience than is tolerable to elite critics of society. What violence may express in movies will be our main interest in what follows, but it will be necessary, too, to discuss the general framework of the mass media of which movies are a part. One of the interconnecting themes among the different popular arts is given by Damon Knight in a discussion of science fiction: "A basic premise of all pulp fiction, from which magazine science fiction is derived, is that only the fear of imminent, violent death can make the human psyche function at its full intensity."[8] Violence as motivation gives the maximum definition to a story, a principle common to magazine fiction and violent movies.

One of the films that I saw in England and which contributed to my later recognition of America was *I Walk Alone,* 1947. Here is James Agee's contemporary review of the film: "Good performances by Wendell Corey and Kirk Douglas; a sharp scene about an old-fashioned gangster's helplessness against modern business methods. Some better than ordinary night-club atmosphere. Otherwise the picture deserves, like four out of five other movies, to walk alone, tinkle a little bell, and cry 'Unclean, unclean.' "[9] Agee begins by noting, accurately and professionally, nice details in the film and then, for no reason given in the review, puts it down severely with his joke on the title. Twenty years later Andrew Sarris found a little more to say for it; discussing

the director Byron Haskin, he counted *I Walk Alone* as one of several "genre films all with unexpected deposits of feeling and comedy."[10] There is a link between Agee's and Sarris's views: Agee consigns the film to the eighty percent of films that are routine, commercial, popular, and Sarris does so, too, but discriminates more patiently within the heap. Agee was constantly unsatisfied as he sat through the popular films of the 40s and hankered for the films of the 30s. However, *I Walk Alone,* and other movies of the second half of the 40s, are the first movies I saw that I still remember, and they existed for me without Agee's burden of aesthetic assumptions formed by other films.

The period is one that has a contested reputation. For example, André Bazin has proposed that "by 1938 or 1939 the talking film, particularly in France and in the United States, had reached a level of classical perfection as a result, on the one hand, of the maturing of different kinds of drama developed in part over the past ten years inherited from the silent film, and, on the other, of the stabilization of technical progress."[11] If this is accepted as a faithful judgment of the late 30s, it follows that the later developments must be post-classical. Extending the morphology of styles implicit in Bazin's formula, the movies I grew up with were baroque, Hellenistic, overblown, late. No one has contributed more than Bazin to an understanding of postwar films, by his analysis of camera movement as a substitute for cutting, for example, but his belief in a classical norm opposes this insight. The consequence of an idea that movies have an optimum balance of techniques, a correspondence of length and plot development, can be seen in Manny Farber's important article "Underground Films."[12] Writing in 1957 he defined B films (crisp, small-screen, black-and-white movies) as the real arena of Hollywood, and "underground" in their resistance to prestige production values of color, big screen, monster stars, or, indeed, box-office success. Implicit in Farber's stand, with his admiring references to 30s prototypes, is a taste for a compact, speedy, laconic style. One can enjoy these qualities without considering them the only virtuous means. Though underground films, in Farber's sense, continue through the 40s and 50s, it is primitivistic to admire only them. The feature movies of the 40s and 50s, especially in the films of violence, reveal thematic complexity as well as formal elaboration. This is, and very significantly, the period in which the feature movie became both intense and "maximized."

I take this word from E. R. Curtius, who, in discussing topics of consolatory oratory in ancient Greece, observed: "among the personages of Greek mythology there was no mortal more aged than Tithonus. But was there among them someone who died in earliest youth, and hence, like Tithonus, represents a maximum? Yes, the infant Archemorus (the Greek name means 'dying in the beginning')."[13] That is to say, these types symbolized, with singular force, senility or early death. In the movies we are faced with figures that embody in terms of contemporary references maximum states of age, beauty, strength, revenge, or whatever. The theme of sergeants is an example of the maximized type (in this case, a leader, but a man of the people, an intimate authority, as it were). In *I Walk Alone,* Burt Lancaster is an ex-convict but a loyal friend with a code of honor; by contrast Kirk Douglas is socially acceptable but faithless and corrupt. The two men are maximized symbols, one, as Agee pointed out, for old-fashioned entrepreneurial élan (Lancaster as good bootlegger), and one for modern executive skills (Douglas as corrupt behind a corporate shield). Both attitudes to business (i.e., life) are appropriate in the "capitalistic" United States. Equally, the nightclub, the object for which the men fight, is realistic in terms of American sociology as a place of nocturnal leisure, an urban 20th-century equivalent of the Machiavellian courts of Elizabethan revenge tragedy.

The films treated in this book are largely the movies I saw as a consumer, paying for my seat, and any aesthetic that emerges should, in my opinion, hold onto its source in the original act of moviegoing. The critical notions to be discussed are not those I had as a regular, not to say compulsive, moviegoer, but I do not want to lose that early feeling, the capacity for identification, that made me see *I Walk Alone* several times when it was first released. When I cite a writer like Curtius, or, as later, Erwin Panofsky, it is because the popular culture of which movies are a part needs to be seen in a context of genres and types. Film criticism provides little precedent for this, whereas literary criticism and art history contain relevant ideas.

Any reading or decoding of *I Walk Alone* can best be done in terms of a context of related movies. In the film, for instance, Lizabeth Scott, like the disputed club, belongs to Kirk Douglas, but she gravitates to Burt Lancaster when she finds that fifty percent of the club is morally his. This is not a calculating move but a moral response, and one that implicates the *mise en scène* in the human maneuvers. Similarly the gambling casino in *Desert Fury,* 1947, is a symbolic area for both Lizabeth Scott and Mary Astor. Gambler John Hodiak intends a two-

generation sexual conquest, and for her daughter's protection as well as from jealousy, Mary Astor bans Lizabeth Scott from the casino that she owns and that is, of course, common ground with Hodiak. This is not to propose a quasi-Freudian symbolism linking architecture and the female body, but rather to show the reciprocal economy of the action of the plot and the scene in which it occurs. These two correspondences of women and architectural scene are echoed in other movies of the period, and such confirmations are necessary for accurate reading.

Essential to the discussion of movies is a sense of normal images and recurrent themes, whereas the most enthusiastic appreciations of popular movies have been oriented another way. In the absence of any disciplined traditional forms of film criticism, writers have appropriated popular movies as if they were found objects removed from their original context and assigned lavish and arbitrary significance. Raymond Durgnat provides an example of the out-of-context overanalysis of the popular film in his discussion of a good science-fiction film *This Island Earth,* 1955. He is undoubtedly correct when he writes that "the emotional and moral 'catchment-area' of an apparently 'escapist' film may be far more extensive, and realistic, than its overt content."[14] However, when he discovers in this one film links "between an unconscious conflict, certain cultural stereotypes, a philosophy of violence, and cold war attitudes,"[15] we are entitled to consider this as insight run riot. His basic interests are cultural and social here but handled with a freedom that is similar to Parker Tyler's earlier use of reverie and psychoanalysis as the basis of film criticism. Tyler analyzed popular movies in terms "of dreams, half-remembered associations of our past, or subconscious or conscious literary memories. The fact that we are so physically relaxed in our theater seats corresponds to our effort to woo the visual blank of sleep . . . "[16] What interests me however in, say, Lizabeth Scott films, are those properties specific to popular movies which can be validated by comparison with other films and other mass media. Tyler's approach resists proof, and Durgnat, in the article cited, is applying too many prior notions of America to a single American product.

The definition of the audience for movies is a necessary part of any discussion of popular films. It has been stated so often that the audience at the movie theater is passive that references are unnecessary. Why document a cliché? The assumption is that the perceptual processes involved at the movies are less demanding than those required in see-

I Walk Alone, Paramount Pictures Corp.

Top, *The Lineup,* Columbia Pictures Corp.
Bottom, *Desert Fury,* Paramount Pictures Corp.

ing a play or reading a book. In fact, the faculties engaged in watching the movies are similar to those in reading any other sign system. To start with, the spectator is taking in a complex spectacle of combined visual, verbal, musical, and natural sound elements. Emphasis can shift from one or two of these levels to others, as with long shots of activity without words; music may be used thematically to designate people or events and as a bridge between discrete sequences. Both uses of music have been criticized by defenders of a visually-based pure aesthetic of cinema, but both musical usages must be considered options within the whole texture of a film. As the various elements exchange dominance, we must define a film as a total of visual and sonic levels rather than isolate one level from the mixture. Even when we are being soothed by mood music, it is by an intricately coordinated progression of separate techniques.

There is a sense in which the audience is strongly present in a movie, not only during the screening but also in its formative stages. To get financial backing for a film the producer needs to be able to define the interests of an audience not less than a year in the future; to make the film usually requires several months work at the least. As the producer's time sense is being applied to the future tastes of a statistically defined audience, he needs evidence that his theme has durability through production time. Since a good many feature films are planned to make most of their money at the time of their first release, film-makers are confronted with a difficult problem. Like car stylists, film-makers have to work for the satisfaction of a half-known future audience. The position of both Detroit and Hollywood resembles that of the speculative builders who erected the majority of New York townhouses; they were built for hypothetical clients on the gamble that changes in demand and taste would occur more slowly than the completion of the products. This is one source of the extraordinary quality that films have of being topical while being at the same time conservative and folkloric. A successful film representing a mutation of a current convention will be imitated because it introduces vital information about previously unknown audience interests.

To work for the near future, you have to extrapolate present successes into probable future trends, and you must protect your film against obsolescence during production. Fashions in the movies reveal the problem clearly; they are glamorous but not too precisely datable. In the 40s clothes for women were often poised in a strange region of use, somewhere between negligee and ball gown. It took a long time for mini-skirts to get into movies, as designers waited to see if the style would endure long enough for girls in films to wear them without looking out-of-date by release time. (The first mini-skirted heroine in a feature was, not unexpectedly, English: Susannah York in *Kaleidoscope,* 1966.) Box-office receipts are both a guide to present taste and a basis for projecting future enterprises. Film critics often deplore the importance of the box office to movie-makers, as if it showed what a venal affair film-making is, but movies are a mass art and must be acceptable to a mass audience. Hence, our reactions as a group have to be, so far as possible, anticipated when we see a new popular film.

Fan magazines during the 50s continued to provide background information about film stars (only stars and actors; other Hollywood technicians are out of sight) as they had done earlier. The information is neither critical nor descriptive; it is a view of the stars' real life as shaped by their current roles and by crossovers between their leisure and their working images. The information is part gossip, part iconography. It is both a guide to the taste and attitudes of the readers (part of the film audience) and a conditioning of that audience. For instance, in "Love Is a Gamble," an article ascribed to Barbara Stanwyck, the actress discussed her current role: "In 'Thelma Jordan' I play a woman who is a desperate gambler. . . . Acting the part of a bewildered, unbalanced woman doesn't mean I agree with or approve such females. I most certainly do not. But they're challenging and interesting roles to play. They're exciting escapism for me as well as for the audience."[17] From this the article goes on to become a homiletic piece about life in general and concludes: "I'm no crusader—no moralizer. But sometimes I think that maybe one or more of the unhappy women I often play in pictures will hold a mirror to some woman movie-goer—dent herself into seeing herself as those around her do."[18] In the same magazine is a picture story of Lizabeth Scott whose "idea of fun is to rush off early in the morning to the antique shops, then spend a busy afternoon working at re-finishing and re-painting her new purchases."[19] In the photographs she looks and dresses as she does in current movies (both she and Stanwyck were under contract to Hal Wallis at the time). In another fan magazine a story about Marilyn Maxwell begins: "The one-time vocalist with Buddy Rogers' band who came into prominence as Kirk Douglas' shady sweetheart in *Champion* was (before her marriage) referred to by jealous Hollywood ladies as 'the female Errol Flynn.' "[20] This single sentence compresses a great deal of show business information including "learned" refer-

Top, *The Big Heat,* Columbia Pictures Corp.
Bottom, *Thelma Jordan,* Paramount Pictures Corp.

Top, *Out of the Past,* RKO Radio Pictures.
Bottom, *Desert Fury,* Paramount Pictures Corp.

Man in the Shadow, Universal Pictures.

ences to pop music, a movie, male actors, and a sexual implication made very plain.

Thus when somebody who has read a piece on Marilyn Maxwell, or comparable items on other actors and stars, goes to the movies the character is already familiar. This kind of cross-media information is less widely distributed now than it used to be, but the self-referring pattern of the mass media continues in more scattered forms with articles on entertainers, product endorsement, fashion modeling, advertising, items in gossip columns, appearances on television, fund raising, and so on. It is a standard practice to compare film stars with history or art history, and occasionally it is illuminating, as when a color photograph of Jeff Chandler was captioned "a Roman warrior in faded dungarees."[21] His blocky torso, his carven head, the solid hair, were like what one means by Roman portraiture, while the Americanness of his style—"faded dungarees"—was incontestable. At any rate the image characterizes vividly his roles as an obdurate and patient hero, tough and undemonstrative. Characteristically Chandler's personal production, Drango, 1957, deals with the problems of a serious Union officer trying to administer an occupied Southern town after the War Between the States.

Gustave Le Bon wrote that "the art of appealing to crowds is no doubt of an inferior order, but it demands quite special aptitudes. It is often impossible on reading plays to explain their success. Managers of theaters when accepting pieces are themselves, as a rule, very uncertain of their success, because to judge the matter it would be necessary that they should be able to transform themselves into a crowd."[22] Flair is still needed but Le Bon's ironic comment, written at the end of the 19th century, has been partially realized. Film producers have developed the techniques to anticipate future audiences. They have become as a crowd.

Three sources of audience information are available to moviemakers: (1) box-office receipts, supplemented by market research; (2) profiles of the different genres and knowledge of the present state of a convention; and (3) surrogates of the public within the production team itself. The first is a feedback from audience to studio which, if properly interpreted, will provide information for future decisions. The second is basically a historical appraisal of the level of topicality enjoyed by set situations at a given moment (what is the status of boxing movies, prison movies, rock 'n' roll musicals, or whatever?). The third factor has been investigated by Herbert J. Gans in terms of what he calls "the audience-image." This image is the hypothetical form of the audience for whom, in the absence of a live audience, one is working. The making of films is a group operation in which numerous specialists have areas of authority; thus the production staff will include live representatives of the future audience. The public is not an undifferentiated mass, of course, but an aggregate of special interests and attitudes. Some of the subcultures that make up the audience are likely to be represented on the set and in a position to influence decisions in terms of their audience-images. Gans cites David Riesman's idea concerning the camera crew: "Since these people are involved in the instrumental, rather than the substantive aspects of movie-making, and in their own leisure choices are more like the rest of the audience than others involved in the production, they may provide the creators with the earliest preview of the validity of their audience-images."[23]

The proper point of departure for a film critic who is going to write about the movies is membership in the large audience for whom they are intended. You need to be in the target area, whereas the majority of film reviewers write as a hostile minority interested primarily in works that are above obsolescence. The emphasis in this book is on a description of popular movies, viewed in sets and cycles rather than as single entities. It is an approach that accepts obsolescence and in which judgments derive from the sympathetic consumption of a great many films. In terms of continuing themes and motifs, the obsolescence of single films is compensated for by the prolongation of ideas in film after film. The routine of movie-going is, therefore, the base of any criticism of popular movies.

Top, *The Naked Spur,* Metro-Goldwyn-Mayer, Inc.
Bottom, *The Steel Helmet,* Lippert Pictures.

Hollywood 1946–1964

The period covered by this book, 1946–1964, has a legible identity in the history of Hollywood, but this does not mean that it is simply defined. The period was one of stress and of reaction to stress, but such pressures for change are normal in the technological media. During the 40s the visual quality of both black-and-white and color film stock and of sound-recording equipment improved, changes that were smooth extensions of existing techniques. Light and sound were clarified, but their functions were unchanged. In 1953, in response to the competition of television, known but shelved techniques for photographing a big image were introduced. New equipment was needed, and the redesign of cinema prosceniums followed, changes that were discontinuous with previous technical levels. Before the introduction of the big screen the standard ratio was 1:1.22; CinemaScope takes a screen of 1:2.33, and the new standard ratio has stretched horizontally to 1:1.66.

The year 1946 was a peak in the post-war boom: "with its gross takings of $1750 million [it] was the most profitable year in the industry's history."[24] Productivity was still high in 1948, a year in which Hollywood produced 366 movies which were seen by an estimated audience of 70 million a week.[25] Then there was a reduction of foreign earnings owing to new tax regulations in Britain, and a Federal anti-trust action separated the studios from their domination of theater chains. Breaking the link between production and distribution coincided with the growing threat of television. Hollywood's response included an economy drive, and one result of this was a number of spare, tightly planned movies of which *High Noon,* 1952, is the best remembered. Such economies had been rehearsed earlier in the 40s, during wartime, and had had the effect of product streamlining. This continued after World War II as a move toward outdoor locations, which has been attributed to the influence of Italian neo-realism but was more probably caused by the need for economies in building sets. It is noticeable, for example, that an increase in efficient scripting accompanied American documentary visual style. What happened is that various iconographic themes of American movies were enacted in non-studio settings. The popularity of outdoor shooting also reduced the formal stylization, often exquisite in its graduated artificiality, by which the major studios could be identified in the 30s and early 40s. I can remember that Warner films had the best fogs and Paramount's the best whitewood suburb; RKO had the house built for *The Magnificent Ambersons* in 1942, and it showed up in subsequent movies, including *The Fallen Sparrow* of the following year.

Another problem for the studios was created by the stars, who, as their long-term contracts expired, did not renew them with the major studios whose tyrannies they remembered only too well. In the 50s the stars could negotiate from individual strength; most of them earned larger salaries for appearing in the same kind of films they had starred in before, but updated in terms of more sophisticated audience-expectations and their own greater age. Although the monolithic structure of the major studios was breaking down, neither the independent stars nor the proliferating independent producers wanted to change the popular base of movies. For all its troubles, Hollywood in the period 1946–1964 produced films that can be regarded as a continuation of the traditional movies. The star system, the combination of schematic narrative with spatial illusionism, the entanglement of topical incidents with recurrent situations—in some respects it is the period of the maximum development of these factors. The films of the period, for all their adaptations to the new crises, found forms in which to maintain the impact and confidence of earlier movies even as a shift in mass communications was modifying Hollywood's authority.

Not everybody views the period from the end of World War II until the early 60s as a legible historical unity. Charles Higham and Joel Greenberg argue for the 40s as "the apotheosis of the U.S. feature film, its last great show of confidence and skill before it virtually succumbed artistically to the paralyzing effects of bigger and bigger screens, the collapse of the star system."[26] It is true that the star system no longer existed in its unquestioned imperial form, but there were still plenty of gossip columns and fan magazines devoted solely to mass-media heroes. Incidentally, the origin of the star system was in the demand of early audiences for names as opposed to stock labels for their favorite players. Not satisfied with anonymous typological figures, they wanted *named* typological figures; this situation has not fundamentally changed.

The use of the word "paralysis" shows that Higham and Greenberg equate big screen movies with static spectacle and, conversely, small-screen movies, especially black-and-white ones, with faster cutting, which they regard as more cinematic. It is true that the big cambered panoramic screen was expected by its critics to lose intimacy by endless medium shots, to make audiences dizzy if the camera moved quickly, and to be diffuse and non-dramatic in lighting. The first CinemaScope movies used the new space tentatively or, as in *How to Marry a Millionaire,* 1953, diagrammatically: the players reclined when possible to fill the horizontal screen or were spread about vast apartments self-sufficient or detached as cats. In fact, in the second year of CinemaScope, 1954, the problems of lighting were brilliantly solved in *Hell and High Water,* and camera movements became free and mobile in *Vera Cruz,* 1954,[27] which had the first vertical downward shot on the big screen. This development culminated in *A Star Is Born,* 1954, with its rapid cutting, camera movements, and light changes.

It is estimated that the United States now has a weekly film audience of about 40 million, 30 million fewer than twenty years ago. In 1968, 180 American-made films were released, but many of these were not filmed in the United States. Recently, at a time when there were 72 films in production, 43 were being shot abroad, 13 were on locations in this country, and only 15 were actually being made in Hollywood.[28] The fact that a film is displaced for practical reasons from Southern California does not mean that it ceases to be American popular art, however, any more than the lower audience figure denies the status of a mass art.

The pressure on Hollywood as a system started, then, in the 40s, but it was not until the 60s that it introduced a real change in popular culture. There is today a different pattern of consumption that has brought a more varied distribution system into operation. Jerry Wald has been quoted as saying in the late 50s that "Mass audiences are hep now; there are 25 million college graduates. There's no such thing as highbrow and lowbrow any more."[29] The once absolute distinction between commercial and avant-garde films, between Hollywood and foreign movies, between art and exploitation films, has been eroded. This is due both to the pulverization of the monolithic industry and to the more instructed audiences referred to by Wald. Multiplying college film societies and the late shows on television have brought more of the past of the cinema into public view than was ever available before in the United States. There are now at least two generations of audiences brought up in the discriminating consumption of films. It is relevant here to mention one of the crossovers that take place between what used to be distinct areas of film-making, between different cultural levels. Jean-Luc Godard's *Alphaville,* 1965, used the narrative and stylistic conventions of the private-detective movie to argue human versus non-human values. The film opens with Lemmy Caution reading a book of poems by Paul Eluard which may be an ironic but purposeful reference to one of the films in the genre Godard is miming. In the movie *Kiss Me Deadly,*

1955, Mike Hammer puzzles over a Christina Rossetti poem which acts as message and clue.

As abundance lessened, diversity increased. Traditional forms no longer have the built-in momentum, the automatic allure, of a few years back. Francois Truffaut has argued that "the James Bond series . . . is nothing else than a rough caricature of all of Hitchcock's work, and of *North by Northwest* in particular."[30] Undoubtedly the nonchalance and extremism of the Bond films are influenced by *North by Northwest,* 1959, but this is because, of all Hitchcock's work up to that date, it is the one most in phase with the recent taste for relaxed structure and a glamorous, offhand *mise en scène.* This particular film of Hitchcock's was useful to the Bond film-makers because it was itself part of the new taste. The ironies and double takes of recent detective and spy films were engaging at first but later became facetious and predictable, as in *Modesty Blaise,* 1966, where the jokes arise from a basic lack of confidence in the story line. There is another way to handle no longer authoritative conventions, and that is by emphasizing a potential half realized in earlier movies but not previously fulfilled. The Westerns made by Sergio Leone in Italy from 1964 revived the genre by the new magnitude of slaughter. Based on a mastery of the American Western, he expanded action to the high pitch of violence characteristic of Japanese Samurai films. The original *The Seven Samurai,* 1954, directed by Akira Kurosawa, was remade by John Sturges in Hollywood as *The Magnificent Seven,* 1960, but Sturges failed to catch the cruel edge of Kurosawa. Leone, however, succeeded in uniting the two forms. Only after this was Samuel Peckinpah's *The Wild Bunch,* 1969, able to cope with violence of Italo-Japanese intensity.

Another factor that may be mentioned in the transformation of the popular cinema is the return of fast cutting. Cuts are frequently no longer as smooth as possible but are conspicuously discontinuous: it is as if Soviet montage has been revived via television commercials. Cutting like this creates a different space and, indeed, a different time from that produced by the maintenance of continuous action. In short, we may have reached the close of the period defined by André Bazin as beginning with Jean Renoir's "search after composition in depth which is, in effect, a partial replacement of montage by frequent panning shots and entrances. It is based on a respect for the continuity of dramatic space and, of course, of its duration."[31] Hence Cinema-Scope films can be viewed as a logical development of this aesthetic of flowing space. The recent

Top and bottom, *The Tattered Dress*, Universal Pictures.

Top, *House of Bamboo.* Bottom, *Warlock.*
Both films·Twentieth Century-Fox Film Corp.

film of stepped-up violence relies on cutting, so that a gunfight, for instance, becomes an anthology of stances, wounds, falls, made tolerable to the public by not dwelling on bullet impact (except for glimpses of galvanic body reactions) or exit wounds (except for glimpses of torn clothing and spurts of arterial blood).

Although the production of new genre films is restricted today, earlier genre films are still accessible. To confine ourselves to violent subjects, films of the later 40s and 50s are still psychologically close to spectators in the last third of the century. It is not axiomatic that it should be so, because there is an historical cut-off point at which recent styles of fashion and industrial design, as of movies, become remote without becoming aestheticized. It is an experience of the recent past in which familiar objects in the environment solidify into alien configurations. On the whole this has not yet happened to the postwar American film of violence. It is still a part of general taste, embodied elsewhere in the styling of American automobiles, which have not fundamentally altered during the same period. The annual style changes were sufficient to entertain us with a comedy of newness but not radical enough to disrupt continuity with earlier models.

What are the constants that enable us to view postwar violent movies on pretty much the same terms as when they were made, even though we have changing expectations of new films? One factor is a cynical attitude toward people and organizations, deriving in part from the experiences of servicemen in World War II. Related to this sophistication, expressed in both situations and dialogue, is a willingness to accept non-upbeat victories within the happy ending required of most genre movies. In *Ramrod,* 1947, for instance, just about everybody is killed except for the hero and the woman who caused the trouble; she recoils from the carnage, and the hero, seeing her clear, at last, withdraws from her. Another influential factor is psychoanalysis, which was highly influential on literature and the fine arts between the wars and which affected Hollywood after World War II. Its importance is less in the specific appearance of analysts and their couches than in widely shared assumptions about character and motive. Conventions for depth were added to the flatter stereotypes of earlier movies; characters could be either overdetermined or pessimistically unexplained. In either case the inference of complexity, of possessed and haunted intelligence, is inescapable. At the time that the hero acquired memories, insomnia, and compulsions, villains acquired a naturalistically phased abnormality, a primal roughness. Another factor is the vernacular existentialism that thrived in violent movies of the later 40s, deriving from the Resistance formulation of Jean-Paul Sartre, that is to say, the action-oriented version of the philosophy. Sartre's admiration for tough American writers just made his ideas more sympathetic. *Brute Force,* 1947, for example, uses a prison the way Sartre used a room in hell and a concentration camp as images of the human state. It is not the dogmatic use of the skepticism, the popular psychoanalysis, or the vernacular existentialism in particular films that is significant; it is their combined diffuson that turned the prewar action film (basically athletic and cheerful) into the more savage, more pessimistic film of violence with its gallery of extreme situations and desperate heroes.

No one film can be identified as the first film of new violence, but there is an accumulation of films sufficient to set the changed mood. Before listing a cluster of anticipatory movies, however, here are some descriptions of the change. It has been referred to as "the rich melodramatic substratum of the Forties and early Fifties."[32] "Hollywood has spawned, since 1946, a series of ugly melodramas featuring a cruel aesthetic, desperate craftsmanship, and a pessimistic outlook."[33] A reviewer of Andrew Sarris observed that he seemed strongest in discussing "directors who exhibit perverse moral complexities in the form of melodrama—Aldrich, Sirk, Phil Karlson."[34]

During World War II there were various films in which the hero or heroes died. In *Bataan,* 1943, the heroes' final satisfaction is not survival but a costly defeat, taking large numbers of Japanese soldiers with them when they died. In *13 Rue Madeleine,* 1946, James Cagney as an American secret agent does not escape the Nazis but holds out under torture until they and he are destroyed in a pre-arranged bombing raid. War films are a special case, it is true, because patriotic deaths have a built-in consolatory affect. However, in a film of 1945 the title itself, *They Were Expendable,* declares a notion of human life as not an absolute value. The film deals with a delaying action in the Pacific, the heroes of which are nonessential. Here is an example of the sophistication about institutions, in this case the Navy, that I mentioned earlier. The mortality of men in war is matched by the increased vulnerability of heroes and also by their contaminated origins. A film of 1942, *This Gun for Hire,* is apposite here: Alan Ladd plays the central character, a hired killer in the role that made him a star. This is an early example of popular culture's adoption of the anti-hero. In *The Glass Key,* of the same year, Ladd moved from anti-hero to hero, though of an amoral sort. The central point of the latter film is his beating up (including a swollen face and shuffling walk), an episode treated at more length than was customary at the time. In *The Fallen Sparrow,* 1943, John Garfield played an early neurotic hero (sweaty face, trembling hands), hounded by memories of his torture in prison after the Spanish Civil War. The hero has a past which is the source of his vulnerability. In 1946 Burt Lancaster's role in *The Killers* expanded the theme of the vulnerable hero: his part is that of one of the most elaborate losers in the whole dark genre. Losing on this scale has a paranoid grandeur in its conspiratorial and threatening completeness.

This is the period of the fall guy (that is, the man to be framed), a term first connected with two films from Dashiell Hammett novels. In *The Maltese Falcon,* 1941, the character proposed for framing is a minor gunman, but in *The Glass Key* framing is in the foreground as a technique of the hero's. The psychological consequence of framing is to convert society into an unreliable and malicious place in which guilt can be manipulated and assigned to sacrificial victims. It is the civilian equivalent of expendability. There are, so to say, obscure tyrants dealing in false reputations and hidden violence. The late 40s has the most spectacular of these, including *Dark Corner,* 1946, *Out of the Past,* 1947, *Dark Passage,* 1947, *The Lady from Shanghai,* 1948, and *D.O.A.,* 1949. The fall guy is in theory the innocent bystander, but there is a new emphasis on the ambiguity of the line between innocence and guilt and on the danger of arbitrary classification. Associated with this is the shakiness of a society that tolerates these masquerades. And, of course, the term *fall* guy is rich in pessimistic implications.

Late in the 40s Richard Widmark's career developed in a comparable way to Ladd's, from success in the part of a psychopathic killer in *Kiss of Death,* 1947, and a hoodlum in *Street with No Name,* 1948, to the neurotic good guy of *Halls of Montezuma,* 1950, and *The Frogmen,* 1951. By 1952 Manny Farber could describe Widmark "as probably the only literate, salty-talking he-man."[35] Widmark's career is far less stereotyped than Ladd's, but common to both actors are their emergence from villain to hero roles and their extension of tensions and violence into the formerly more placid postures of the hero figure.[36] The cumulative effect of such actors and films was to expose audiences to the spectacle of violence and death in a context of psychic depth, institutional doubt, and existential solitude.

During the 40s and 50s a new generation of directors appeared, among them Robert Aldrich, Budd Boetticher, Delmer Daves, Edward Dmytryk, Samuel Fuller, Anthony Mann, Nicholas Ray, and Donald Siegel. These men had in common the fact that they accepted the overall conventions of action movies but transformed the handling of violence from within: greater intensity and greater naturalism developed simultaneously. The age of these directors spans twelve years: the oldest, Anthony Mann, was born in 1906, the youngest, Robert Aldrich, in 1918. By comparison their films are usually more urgent, more tense, than those of William Dieterle, Allan Dwan, Henry King, Lewis Milestone, Raoul Walsh, and William Wellman, all of whom were born before 1900. The directors of the older generation responded, in one film or another, to the new mode. Dieterle's *The Turning Point,* 1952, Dwan's *Sands of Iwo Jima,* Milestone's *Halls of Montezuma,* Walsh's *White Heat,* 1949, Wellman's *Yellow Sky,* 1948, have the characteristic edge. None of these directors equaled the adaptability of Henry Hathaway with his *House on 92nd Street,* 1945, *Call Northside 777,* 1948, both documentary-style thrillers, or *Kiss of Death,* 1947, and *Rawhide,* 1951, both of which have foreground-hulking psychopaths. In 1951 Hathaway made *Desert Fox,* remarkable only for its opening sequence, a British commando raid on Rommel's headquarters, designed to destroy everybody in it in the hope of hitting Rommel. The quantity of surprise deaths prefigures later levels of violence. Henry King's contribution to the new genre is less *The Gunfighter,* 1950, than a later work, a bizarre revenge film with a procession of assassinations, *The Bravados,* 1958.

Despite the frequent identification of movies by director, the primary influence may be that of the producer. Between 1946 and 1950, Hal Wallis produced five films with as many directors: *The Strange Love of Martha Ivers, Desert Fury, I Walk Alone, Thelma Jordan,* and *Dark City,* directed respectively by Lewis Milestone, Lewis Allen, Byron Haskin, Robert Siodmak, and William Dieterle. Undoubtedly sufficient expertise can discriminate one director's style, or touch, from the others, but the dominant and shaping influence is Wallis's. The films are a substantial part of the postwar cycle of dark films, dealing with complicated relationships that push characters into or out of crime. Between 1950 and 1958 another producer, Aaron Rosenberg, made eight Westerns: *Winchester 73, Bend of the River, The Man from the Alamo, The Far Country, Man Without a Star, Backlash, Night Passage,* and *The Badlanders.* Here the directors are Anthony Mann (the first two), Budd Boetticher,

Mann again, King Vidor, John Sturges, James Neilson, and Delmer Daves. As a last example there is the work of Albert Zugsmith, who produced, between 1955 and 1960, a group of what Universal-International called "modern dramas": *Female on the Beach, Written on the Wind, The Tattered Dress, Man in the Shadow, Touch of Evil,* and *High School Confidential* (the latter distributed by Metro-Goldwyn-Mayer). Whatever Douglas Sirk brought to the glamorous and nervy *Written on the Wind,* whatever George Zuckerman's scripts gave to it and to *The Tattered Dress,* the fact remains that Zugsmith's is the linking personality in all these films that flash along the interface of bright society and the underworld. Like the earlier group by Wallis, these films center on the threshold of legality and crime.

Writing about the action films that show in double bills on the bright strip that runs across America from 42nd to Market Street, Manny Farber praised as "the true masters of the male action film—such soldier-cowboy-gangster directors as Raoul Walsh, Howard Hawks, William Wellman, William Kieghley, the early, pre-*Stagecoach* John Ford, Anthony Mann."[37] He showed admiration, too, for younger directors, for "The Aldrich films . . . filled with exciting characterizations—by Lee Marvin, Rod Steiger, Jack Palance—of highly psyched-up, marred, and bothered men."[38] And Farber liked Phil Karlson's "scary cheapness" as in *The Phenix City Story.* His favorite movies are either big productions of the 30s, like the early Cagney films, or B films of the 40s, which are comparable in duration and pungency to the features of the 30s. "The underground directors have been saving the American male on the screen for three decades. . . ."[39]

Farber's eye and memory for the original underground films, which he writes about like an aphorist on pep pills, are marvelous, but what about the rest of the argument? His aesthetic is counter to *From Here to Eternity,* 1953, *The Best Years of Our Lives,* 1946, and *Giant,* 1956, which he finds overblown. He dislikes the Westerns of Delmer Daves and James Stewart. He reduces the postwar situation to a choice between lean male movies and gross features. In fact, as feature movies got longer they absorbed some of the gritty verities of the B picture: A and B turned into AB. It is nostalgic to maintain a strictly pure B standard as Farber does. Physical reality can be expressed, as in *Attack!,* almost exclusively by the history of what happens to one man's body (Jack Palance), or it is combinable with more elaborate layers of reference. Postwar tourism reinforces at a factual level the fictional gangster story in *House of Bamboo,* for example;

an American gang, using military techniques, attacks illegally the Japan that America has recently fought and defeated legitimately. Shot on location, it presents the exotic as data. The elaborately scenic style of the James Stewart Westerns is only a "post card" to Farber, but the locations have a function. The West of the 1880s is enacted in the unchanged present landscape, known to us from post cards, photographs in the *National Geographic* magazine, and state tourist-office literature, or from the bubble on a Vista-Dome train and through an automobile windshield. To Farber the peaks and the streams and the forests are fancy additions to the puritan male ethic that he discovers in action films. In fact, they are a part of the correspondences among media which give a film the authority of being real at more than one level as it complies with information derived from other sources. This kind of allusion, characteristic of postwar movies, has an elaborate emblematic quality opposed to Farber's attachment to the straight and narrow.

White Heat, Warner Bros. Pictures, Inc.

The Expendable Gesamt- kunstwerk

André Breton has recalled a film "in which a Chinese who had found some way to multiply himself invaded New York by means of several million self-reproductions. He entered President Wilson's office followed by himself, and by himself, and by himself, and by himself; the President removed his *pince-nez*. This film, which has affected me far more than any other, was called *The Grip of the Octopus*."[40] Everybody adores bizarre inventions like these in which two of the sources of the cinema, vaudeville and folklore, are reaffirmed by naive and wonderful effects. In this spirit Robert Desnos, in an essay on French popular fiction, praised "the illustrated bindings of certain popular novels: *Nick Carter, Sar Dubnotal, Buffalo Bill, Texas Jack*, and especially *Fantômas* . . . an enormously popular factor in Parisian mythology and oneirology."[41] If we think less in the grandiose forms of myth and dream and more in the shorter terms of urban folklore and vaudeville there is much to be said for Desnos's approach. A logbook of marvels does not constitute film criticism, but it can have the charm of peripheral insight. Films are notoriously difficult to describe with a precision comparable to the standard of discussion in other forms of art. This is one of the reasons for the continuation of fantasizing criticism, in which the film is treated as a found object, completely subject to the finder's invention. The history of the cinema, the attention of the spectator, and the properties of the film as a medium all contribute to our uncertainty. Film history, drafted with some confidence in the 30s, has been under revision ever since. The discovery of copies of supposedly lost movies continually stirs up the state of knowledge. Major American companies have few conservationist impulses about their past products, and good prints of even recent films can be very hard to find. And, of course, new films are produced in such numbers that chroniclers are simply overwhelmed.

Though the chronology of the cinema is becoming clearer, doubts about the aesthetic status of the movies are still unresolved. Early supporters of the medium used humanistic criteria of great thoughts and individual authorship to confer the status of art on films. The function of films as entertainment has been persistently denigrated. "The people who make films don't do it to ennoble man: they are there to make money. Consequently, inevitably, they work upon man's lower instincts. . . ."[42] This recent statement of André Malraux's is a succinct version of a widely held prejudice against the mass media. To apply the standards of traditional high art to popular culture, or vice versa, is inevitably unsatisfactory and leads to prescriptive judgments. All of us exist within a general field of communications that includes high and popular art in different zones. The movies constantly provoke the irrelevant criticism of various groups because the medium reaches the members of different subcultures, unlike fine art, which is relatively concentrated.

The conditions of viewing complicate our responses to films still further. A film viewed in a cinema is perceived as light in darkness and sound in silence in a place entered solely for that purpose. The film is overwhelming, and suddenly it is gone. It is linear and outside our control in its progression, an experience unlike the act of reading, in which we can pace our attention and check back on earlier passages. No such access exists in the cinema where we are confronted by an uncheckable spectacle, composed of visual images, narrative situations, and the sonic dimension of speech, natural sound, and music. Quotation or reference is therefore highly approximate owing to the combination of: (1) concentration in the dark; (2) the emotional nature of the spectacle; and (3) the lack of literary text comparable to that of a theatrical play. As a medium films are subject to rapid fading; they have an entropic tendency in excess of most art forms. Apart from the complexity and elusiveness of a movie as an object of attention, the actual physical body of a film is subject to corruption. A poem is much the same in one typeface or another, and a photographic reproduction of a painting can be reasonably iconic, but the quality of what is seen of a film varies from cinema to cinema. Projection is usually good in first-run theaters and unreliable thereafter; a film seen in a drive-in is a very different experience from the same film seen indoors; and on television not only is the visual imagery transformed in appearance, but the film will be cut, often heavily. On television in 1968, for instance, Orson Welles's *The Lady from Shanghai* was shown without Welles's monologue at the picnic comparing his employers to sharks tearing each other apart, though it is a key sequence, linked both verbally and visually with the aquarium scene and the final gunfight among multiple mirrors. The interruption of films by commercials is not simply distracting but has the effect of making films, originally an art of the overwhelming present, seem preexistent and old in comparison to the commercials that are in the temporal foreground.

To all these variables must be added the constant corrosion of the standard product. For example, *The Wild Bunch* was shortened for commercial distribution by the removal of flashbacks that provided motivation for a central character.[43] However, the success of the film was ensured by the excitement of the violence which provided sufficient moment-by-moment activity to overcome the lessening of internal complexity. This, like so many films, is constructed to survive a process of endless shortening. We can propose a principle of *approximate coherence* in which the casual relationships are much less binding than in, for instance, novels owing to the shifts in our attention between one level of sensory data and another. The state of film prints can be linked to printed texts of, say, 16th-century plays in which the omissions and distortions of a crazy stage manager and an illiterate printer cannot be separated from the original form. Revision is contingent and arbitrary in movies and never the second thought of the filmmakers.

Erwin Panofsky, in a fundamental article, long ago pointed out that "the movies organize material things and persons, not a neutral medium. . . . The medium of the movies is physical reality as such . . . eighteenth-century Versailles—no matter whether it be the original or a Hollywood facsimile, . . . the streets of New York in the rain; the physical reality of engines and animals, of Edward G. Robinson and Jimmy Cagney."[44] Robert Warshow, in the best of his articles on the cinema, remains within Panofsky's insight: "No film ever quite disappears into abstraction: what the camera reproduces has almost always on the most literal level the appearance of reality."[45] He points out that "the actor as an object of perception is real and important irrespective of whether we believe in the character . . ."[46] Godard's comments on Jack Palance in *Contempt,* 1963, support this view: "his physical appearance was good and that was sufficient for me. But he wanted to act, too. So with the body he has, in the role he was playing—it wasn't that of a Western bandit—he didn't have to act, just the fact of his being there was already a kind of performance."[47] Alfred Hitchcock observed that "whenever the hero isn't portrayed by a star, the whole picture suffers, you see, because audiences are far less concerned about the predicament of a character who's played by someone they don't know."[48] At the time it was made, 1946, *Notorious* was celebrated for the longest screen kiss, and Hitchcock has commented on it in a way that reveals his awareness of the attraction of photographed reality. ". . . the public, represented by the camera, was the third party to this embrace. The public was being given the great privilege of embracing both Cary Grant and Ingrid Bergman together. It was a kind of temporary *ménage à trois.*"[49] Though his language seems patronizing, Hitchcock accurately expresses the close identification of audiences that is made possible when the impression of physical reality is carried by the presence of known players.

To the film as an absorbing, temporary object of attention, we must add the factor of environmental correspondences, which confirms at another level the illusion of physical reality. Since its medium is photographed reality, a film is a transformation of the spectator's space and the objects in his environment. In *Written on the Wind,* 1956, for instance, the pessimistic story is set in a world of luxury hotels, private planes, polished cars reflecting the porticoes of great houses, and long dinner tables with gleaming silver; the scene of action is the advertisements from *McCall's, The New Yorker,* and *Harper's Bazaar* given reality. The images on screen are always extending to contemporaneous data off screen, slurring into a sociological matrix. It is not only circumstantial detail and spatial plausibility that carry physical conviction to the audience but also images of products and references to other channels of mass communication. Media-echoes, in which different channels corroborate one another, and environmental allusions reinforce the effect of illusion.

By its nature, the film is a *Gesamtkunstwerk* (total-work, unity of arts), the kind of form in which several arts are combined. The origin of the theory of the *Gesamtkunstwerk* is theatrical and derives from Richard Wagner, who created, and provided the theory for, a synthesis of music, literature (libretto), and the visual arts (decor) crystallized in the act of performance. An architecturally based unity succeeded the operatic in later 19th-century art theory; painting and sculpture combined with applied arts and industrial design under the control of architects. The scope of collaboration ranges from dominance by one partner to openly competitive liaisons. Cinema is inarguably a compound form as opposed to painting or poetry in which absolute one-man control is normal. The silent film was a photographed reality, presented in a theater, with verbal insertions, narrative themes, and external musical accompaniment. The addition of intrinsic sound, first musical, then spoken, and then layered combinations of speech, natural sound, and music fulfilled the potential of sensory coordination present in the silent film. Color extended the visual possibilities but did not depart from the orginal premise of films. All subsequent technical changes have amplified sight or sound, but none has proposed a reduction of the film's multi-leveled synthesis.

On the whole, film critics have not viewed the film as a compound art form, as a complex and heterogeneous structure. On the contrary, they have preferred isolating one of the multiple elements and conferring priority on that. There has been, for example, an overemphasis on the visual properties of movies. I say this not because I am indifferent to the visual aspect, but because it is the coexistence of visual and sonic elements that is uniquely cinematic. As in opera, we have to perceive different kinds of stimuli simultaneously, and the verbal and iconographic elements of movies have been neglected owing to the visual bias. This is not the place to attempt a general theory of cinema, but this point needs to be made so that we can consider, among other things, the function of dialogue in movies of the 40s and 50s.

A general feeling exists among film critics that the fewer words the better and that maybe words ought to work contrapuntally against the visual imagery. A typical opinion is that of Truffaut: "whatever is said instead of being shown is lost upon the viewer."[50] I regard this as both incorrect and old-fashioned. When Eisenstein compared montage to ideographs his theory of cinema was supported by the technical state of the then-silent art and by the vitality of the new ideas of montage. At this late date, however, for Truffaut to propose an essentially visual structure for movies is certainly off the point. This approach derives through inertia, from Eisenstein's attempts at a comprehensive film aesthetics parallel to Ezra Pound's effort to objectify Western languages on ideographic, that is to say visual, principles. When the equilibrium of the silent film was upset, first by sound and then by color, a set of prescriptive aesthetics derived from silent films became current. Most of this writing suffers quite simply from having been done too early, but its prestige has lingered in the absence of effective alternatives.

Most of the films of the period under discussion here have copious dialogue, but this fact does not in the least consign them to the status of being illustrations of novels or of being photographed theater. Dialogue in the movies is irreducibly cinematic. A face or faces in close-up talking have no equivalent in theater or novels; groups in medium shots talking are also by definition cinematic. In one the big scale and intimacy, in the other the interrelationships in space are, as photographed reality, entirely unlike other media. Dialogue is essential in a narrative film; its absence is archaistic or a special case, as in the wordless *The Thief*, 1952. Dialogue in the 40s and 50s was dramatically structured as a few quotations may indicate. In all these cases the sentences advance the action or sum up situations with an aphoristic bite. Sententious writing, in which the scenarios of the period abound, characterize the mood of whole films as much or more than they evoke individual character. In *Warlock*, 1959, Dorothy Malone, before sleeping with a man expecting to be killed in the morning, demands, "What do you want? Your whole life in one night." From *Forty Guns*, 1957, "You shot your way across the map." Jeff Chandler, rescued from a beating in an alley, says he heard, "footsteps coming. The footsteps of men from the 20th century" (*The Tattered Dress*, 1957). At Acapulco the puzzled hero says: "I'll take you away. To one of the far places," to which Rita Hayworth replies, "Oh Michael, we're in one of the far places now" (*The Lady from Shanghai*). Lancaster, out of prison, looks at Broadway: "Fourteen years and it's still the same." "It only looks the same," his friend warns him (*I Walk Alone*). In the same film a headwaiter recommends a wine to the ex-convict: "1933 was a very good year, sir" (it is the year Lancaster went to prison). American dialogue was famous for wisecracks, such as "I'm so framed I look like Whistler's mother" (*Dark Corner*), but these quotations, which are fully representative, show that verbal thrust was not restricted to jokes.[51]

Critics have been reluctant to situate the cinema within a field of popular culture and industrialization. The movies have more in common with the history of prints than with the history of painting, for example. Like prints, movies are produced in multiple originals and distributed widely; they are locked to the concept of mass production. A basis for comparison exists, also, in the development of popular novels and plays in the 18th century and in the growth of illustrated magazines of the last century. As a mass-produced popular culture developed, resistance to it was formulated; there has been open conflict between the products of popular culture and the taste of elite groups accustomed to arbitrating all aesthetic matters. We have inherited this antagonism in the 20th century; fine-art-oriented film critics of a naive and absolutist tendency confront, without much pleasure, the highly evolved products of a mass culture.

The elite-versus-mass polarity raises problems even among those without hostility toward popu-

The Last Wagon, Twentieth Century-Fox Film Corp.

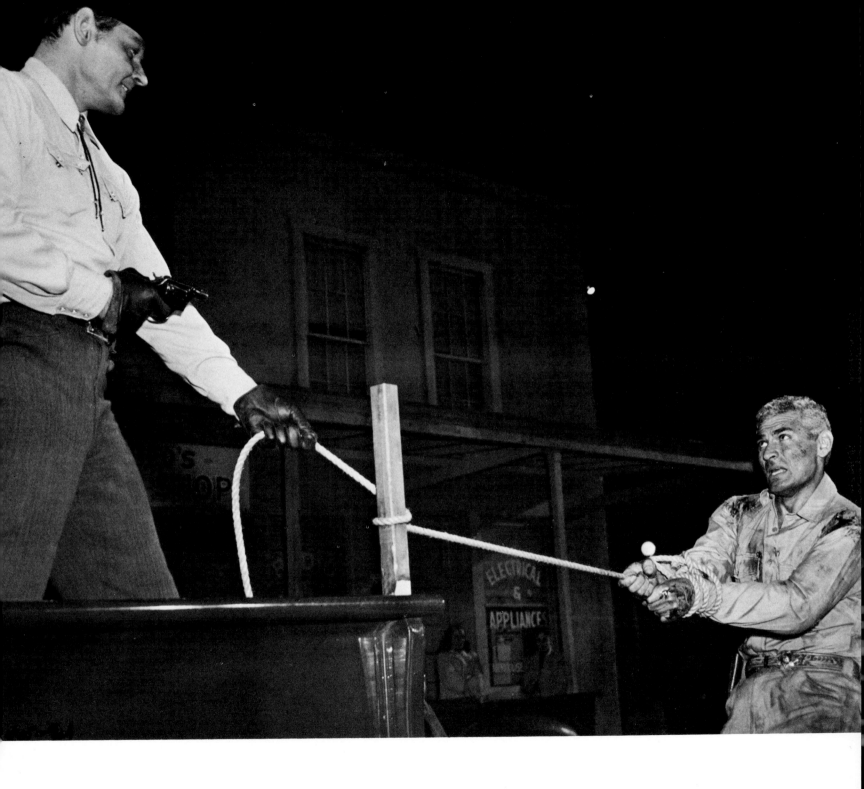

Man in the Shadow, Universal Pictures.

lar culture. Thus Edward A. Shils has proposed three levels of popular culture, each with its appropriate entertainment and aesthetics: superior (or refined) culture, mediocre culture, and brutal culture.[52] All this amounts to no more than a pampered version of the categories of high-, middle-, and lowbrow, and as such, remains divisive and elitist. One way to avoid these limitations would be to consider art on a time scale, in which some works are designed for long-term consumption and some for short-term consumption. To discuss works of art in terms of their temporal function or span of usability has the advantage of allowing a person to operate in all of Shils's grades without conflict.

Thinking in terms of a time scale for art forms makes it possible to take ephemeral art as seriously as the presumptively permanent. A good example is the Art Nouveau poster, of which records remain though many of the originals have perished. It was a mass-produced public art of exceptional sophistication which, after its urban evolution, was distributed along the developing transportation systems that serviced the cities. The posters have iconographic links with other technologies, since they advertised, by means of fantastic and elegant imagery, such products as gas and, later, electric power, bicycles, balloons, automobiles, cigarettes, fountain pens, typewriters, and resort towns.[53] Instead of the ideas of permanence and of enduring masterpieces, derived from traditional literary and art criticism, let us consider expendable art as a historical category.[54] Expendable art is consumed in use; it is operational for intense but short periods. The funeral pyres of Roman emperors were architecture for burning; funeral and commemorative decor thrived in the courts of Europe throughout the 15th, 16th, and 17th centuries. Festival architecture, triumphal processions, colossal sculpture for weddings and ambassadorial receptions, masques, occasional poetry, garden pavilions, decorated arches, fancy costumes—such affairs have been regarded as the symptoms of decadent princes and dukes, but this puritan and unhistorical objection fails to describe the phenomenon. The designs for expendable art were by artists who took temporary displays as seriously as work done for eternity. Movies, in their high topicality, intense participatory appeal, playful expertise, and freedom from a desire to encumber the future with monuments, can be regarded as continuing the tradition of expendable art. Proposal: movies as the court art of mass culture.

The cinema, like the intermezzi at the Court of Ferrara or the masques at the Court of St. James's, can be regarded as an art without monuments. Movies of the early 20th century are fascinating but rather as documents, as relics, than as ongoing works of art. They are more like the bones of a saint in the crypt than the painted altarpiece of his martyrdom in the chapel. The art of the cinema, like that of expendable court art, aims at spontaneous and immediate audience response. A film's temporary domination of spectators is far more complete while it lasts than that elicited by paintings or books. This impact gives films their peculiar power of envelopment. It is hard, however, for a movie with its comparative unconsultability to support afterward the reflective thought that is a property of works of art. Obviously movies can be seen again with pleasure and other benefits, but this is not the same thing as prolonged examination of a compact work. Films are repeatable rather than continuously accessible. Films are most efficient when new, a function that is no less precious, in my view, than the time-binding presence of works of art scheduled for permanence. A film's span of vivid existence is short, like industrial design, fashion in clothes and make-up, advertising, slang, pop music. The survivals of these modes have a period look that works of art, for all their historical causation, do not.

Photographs irrevocably date the sexiest debs and the best-dressed men. Not only does the camera record the physical details of time and place, but the equipment itself is dated by subsequent technical changes that intervene between ourselves and earlier forms of recording. In photographed reality the historical becomes historicist. The consequences of a changing technology are neglected by the supporters of film as a permanent art. Improvements in film stock and lenses, the addition of sound and color to the early mute, black-and-white medium, are embarrassing to film critics with a notion of art as a human activity that transcends hardware. One can speak confidently of technical improvements in photography and sound recording, whereas the emergence of oil paint, gradually replacing tempera, or the move toward chalk as a drawing medium between the 15th and 17th centuries, cannot be described in evolutionary terms. They were changes, but the idea of advancement or improvement does not enter into them.

The cinema, as a combined, technological recording art, is riddled with links to areas of behavior that are highly fugitive: social styles, ways of moving, sexual signals. Speech changes are as conspicuous as shifts in favorite words: for example, Fredric March in movies of the 30s has an English accent, as did other American actors with theater connections or ambitions, but there are no signs of it in March's naturalistic later work. In the movies the extent to which material once absorbing becomes alienated from us is demonstrated constantly. Common to both the science-fiction stories and the movie comedies of the 30s, for instance, is a Depression-stimulated desire for fixed capital and easy money: in science fiction the scientist dreams continually of a privately endowed laboratory or a great invention, and *Mr. Deeds Goes to Town,* 1936, like so many movies of the period, is about a hero's windfall. (Preston Sturges's comedies of the 40s frequently make fun of this situation.) Images of security and of money take less simple forms in the popular arts now. Newspaper reporters were familiar stock figures in movies of the 30s: as roving investigators, these brash and swaggering heroes appeared as projections of working-class immigrant manners into a settled white-collar world. Later, newspaper men in movies are more varied and complex: there are, for instance, Kirk Douglas's ambitious reporter who makes news instead of reporting it in *Ace in the Hole* and James Cagney's alcoholic reporter in *Come Fill the Cup,* both 1951, who files a story on a plane crash headlined "All the Dead Were Strangers." In *Deadline USA,* 1952, Humphrey Bogart played a big city newspaper editor fighting organized crime, and in *Captive City,* 1954, John Forsythe a small-town newspaper editor harassed by local crime. The point is that these newsmen heroes are more subtly motivated and viewed in a more sophisticated relation to institutions than was possible before World War II.

An unsettled problem of film criticism is identification of the unit to be analyzed. There is no comparable problem in art and literary criticism, in which the definition of the limits of works (sonnets, oil paintings, or whatever) and their grouping (by artist, medium, period, school) is substantially agreed on. The problem is not simply the result of the overlapping usage of the terms "cinema," "film," and "movies," which are used here generally as follows: the cinema, meaning films collectively as an art, as a characteristic mode of communication; films meaning particular examples or products; and movies meaning exclusively popular films (Hollywood and all that). When a film critic is faced by a film the usual expedient is to assume that the director's contribution can be counted the basic unit of reference. The extent to which a film reveals the personal characteristics of its director has become the ultimate symbol of value. The director's name is often made to bear an extra-

ordinary weight. Let us consider an example of overloading by quoting Andrew Sarris on Sam Peckinpah: "Unfortunately Peckinpah affects condescending overhead shots in a context reminiscent of Demy's condescension toward Elina Labourdette in *Lola.*"[55] Though one sympathizes with any attempt to analyze kinesthetic effects in films, as an example of directorial expression this is clearly unverifiable.

To propose the director as the sole formative influence is partly a humanistic reflex (one work, one man), and partly a brutal simplification of the conditions of the film as a *Gesamtkunstwerk.* It is meaningful as well as tidy to say of films that they are Hitchcock's or Lang's: here are groups of internally consistent works with recurrent elements that can be validated. Yet other directors, such as Robert Aldrich, Byron Haskin, and Donald Siegel, for all their skills and successes, do not dominate their work with the same authority or with the same degree of interest.

The compulsion to put too much on directors can be taken further by completing Sarris's reference to Peckinpah, who had just completed his second Western, *Ride the High Country,* 1962: "The film represents a fusion of the Boetticher-Scott and Tourneur-McCrea traditions."[56] These "traditions" amount to seven films directed by Boetticher and starring Randolph Scott and a couple of films directed by Jacques Tourneur, starring Joel McCrea *(Stranger on Horseback* and *Wichita,* both 1955). All that Sarris is actually saying is that *Ride the High Country* is structurally of the kind associated with Boetticher, Scott, and in addition Burt Kennedy, writer, and Harry Joe Brown, producer; there being in truth no Tourneur-McCrea line. What had happened, to give a little more detail, is that in 1956 Boetticher, Kennedy, and Scott made *Seven Men from Now,* though with other producers. In the following year Brown joined Scott as co-producer of *The Tall T.* This group of producer, director, writer, and star made two more Westerns *(Ride Lonesome,* 1959, and *Comanche Station,* 1960). These three films were photographed by Charles Lawton, Jr., incidentally. Working with scripts by Charles Lang, Jr., Brown, Boetticher, and Scott made *Decision at Sundown,* 1957, and *Buchanan Rides Alone,* 1958; and in *Westbound,* 1959, Scott and Boetticher were, so to say, on their own. All these films, revolving around the members of the same production group, expanded coherently and inventively the form of the first. They are journey Westerns, over rough country to a remote target or climactic episodes on implied journeys, involving antagonistic people who have to watch each other even as they unite for the journey. (The form is not this group's personal possession, but is found in other films of the period that went in for ambiguous relationships, such as *The Naked Spur,* 1953, and *The Dragoon Wells Massacre,* 1957.) *Ride the High Country* followed this form but with Scott as the villain instead of the hero, a twist that apparently entertained the actor.[57] Sarris knows all this, but his attachment to directors lead him to give Tourneur a consistency he has not shown and to reduce a collaboration of various men to two. Boetticher's earlier and later history as a director, though he is popular with auteur-oriented critics, shows that he operated within this flexible group with a coherence that he has not achieved outside it. The film critic is faced with continually changing alliances of talent rather than with simple pyramids of personal authority.

As it happens, we can indicate, by parallel quotations, possible tensions of a combined art; or, to put it another way, the competitiveness of collaborative roles. Both Hitchcock and Raymond Chandler have recorded their dislike at working with each other on *Strangers on a Train,* 1951, in terms that undoubtedly characterize other collaborations:
"Hitchcock: Whenever I collaborate with a writer who, like myself, specializes in mystery, thriller, or suspense, things don't seem to work out well.
Truffaut: You're referring to Raymond Chandler?
Hitchcock: Right; our association didn't work out at all. We'd sit together and I'd say, 'Why not do it this way?' and he'd answer, 'Well, if you can puzzle it out, what do you want me for?' The work he did was no good and I ended up with Czenzi Ormonde, a woman writer, . . . one of Ben Hecht's assistants."[58]

On September 4, 1950, Chandler wrote of Hitchcock after starting to work for him: "He has a strong feeling for stage business and mood and background, not so much for the guts of the business. I guess that's why some of his pictures lose their grip on logic and turn into wild chases. Well, it's not the worst way to make a picture. His idea of character is rather primitive. Nice Young Man, Society Girl, Frightened Woman, Sneaky Old Beldame, Spy, Comic Relief, and so on."[59] By the end of the month Chandler worried: "It must be rather unusual in Hollywood for a writer to do an entire screenplay without a single discussion with the producer [director?]."[60] On December 7: "I have seen the final script made up from what I wrote, but a good deal changed and castrated. It is, in fact, so bad that I am debating whether to refuse screen credit."[61] On November 10, referring to his

experiences with Billy Wilder on *Double Indemnity,* 1944, as well as with Hitchcock, Chandler summed up the problem of writing in Hollywood: "Too many people have too much to say about a writer's work."[62] The fact that Hitchcock, as might be expected, emerged victorious from this particular agon does not mean he did so simply by virtue of being the director. I give the quotations to indicate the kind of competition that can develop within a group and which at times makes final responsibility hard to locate.

Orson Welles habitually disclaims the released print of his films. Donald Siegel and Joseph Losey, among others, have recorded the recutting of their films, the shifts of meaning that originated with the producer or distributor of their films.[63] An obstinate fact is that much of this spoliation goes unnoticed by the viewers absorbed by the spectacle and momentum of the film as a whole; it certainly is not central to an audience with high tolerance of poor prints. Film aesthetics has suffered from the desire to define films in terms of a compact and homogeneous form, rather than as a compound and heterogeneous one. The form of the popular film is sufficiently flexible to absorb divergent contributions as well as perfunctory resolutions. A comparison might be made with Gothic cathedrals to which, as a rule, no very high criterion of unity can be applied, owing to successive generations of builders, alterations, revivals, and vandalism, all of which have left their traces.[64]

It is not my intention to reduce the importance of directing, but it is necessary to be sure when it is the director who makes the dominant decisions. Particularly in the commercial cinema, the director's control is subject to erosion and to sharing. For example, John Farrow is listed as the director of *Hondo,* 1953, but John Ford also worked on it, and there is no interruption of the attention of anybody following the story. Some actors do more to characterize their films than their directors do. Frank Sinatra's films from 1951 to 1956, all directed by different people, share a single character in successive postures of alienation. This is true of *Meet Danny Wilson,* 1951, *From Here to Eternity, Suddenly,* 1954, and his own production, *Johnny Concho,* 1956, in which he is, respectively, an irritable and aggressive singer, a persecuted soldier, an assassin gunning for the President of the United States, and a humiliated bully. The roles are not single occasions in unique stories but a continuous parade, which must have been Sinatra's satisfaction at the time, as it was what interested his audience. Such continuities can be traced in the movies of actors like Sinatra or Robert Mitchum, Humphrey Bogart or Kirk Douglas, who are much the same in each part. The unity of the actor's roles, the permutations of a fixed identity, are more important than the ability to disappear within different parts, the theoretical test of good theater acting.

John Wayne played Sergeant Stryker in *The Sands of Iwo Jima,* 1949, and Hondo in the film of that name in 1953, one a war film, the other a Western that, at the time, was nicknamed "Wayne's *Shane."* *Hondo* was released a year after *Shane,* and like it deals with the relationship of a man and a boy, and includes a good deal of discussion about guns, growing up, manhood. Both films are basically about initiation, but so is *The Sands of Iwo Jima* in which, as a tough marine sergeant, Wayne first trains the rookies for combat and then leads them ashore and up the mountain. His authority, physically massive, more at ease with men than women on the screen, makes him a natural for action pictures with teaching situations. This pattern persists as late as *The Green Berets,* 1968, in which he convinces a skeptical newsman of the need to fight in Vietnam. Another form of fixed character is indicated by Burt Kennedy: "I wrote a character for Lee Marvin in *Seven Men from Now.* I later put that same character in different situations, the same fun-loving gunfighter, and I think just about every character actor in town played it. Jimmy Coburn, Brian Keith, Richard Boone, Jim Arness."[65]

Male heroes are obviously central to any notes on violence in movies, and one approach to them is by appearance. We can index heroes by the amount of dirt they collect in fighting and running, by the number of their injuries and the length of time needed to heal. High scores are a clear sign of the amount of stress and the intensity of reaction to it. John Wayne and Randolph Scott are usually imperturbable; their clothes, though hard worn, have the comfortable look of favorite work clothes. James Stewart dresses like this, but in the course of Westerns he collects rips that do not mend and injuries that do not heal between sequences. Several Westerns made a point of heroes with injured gunhands: *The Man from Laramie,* 1955, in which Stewart resorts to a rifle balanced on his right forearm when his gun hand is maimed; *The Man from Del Rio,* 1956, in which the hero survives his last walk down the street by bluffing, slowly unbandaging a useless hand; and *Warlock,* in which Widmark, despite an injured hand, draws anyway, though slower than usual. Widmark is repeatedly the battered hero, physically engrossed in his running, falling, frantic postures. In *The Halls of Mon-*

tezuma and *Take the High Ground,* 1953, he introduced into war films his image of the driven man, at the edge of breakdown. In the first he is an officer in combat, in the other a sergeant, mostly in training, a kind of neurotic version of Wayne's solitary Stryker. An influential film in the definition of vulnerable heroes, not above the battle but in the middle of it, was *Twelve O'Clock High,* 1950, which ends with Gregory Peck's breakdown from the strain of command.

The traditional appeal of violence in the popular arts has to do with excitement and shock. To witness the cruelty of villains arousing reciprocal action, to see the power of recovery of brutalized victims, to trace the protracted pattern of stress, is certainly a form of pleasure. The principle of maximization, mentioned earlier in connection with stereotypes, is applicable here: a death is better than a scratch, just as love is better than kindness in terms of narrative situations. It is a matter of what generates intensity. It is relevant to refer to Elizabethan revenge tragedy at this point, for it too exceeded the classically licensed boundaries of moderate violence. Mario Praz points out that it was Seneca who "supplied the Elizabethan dramatists with a justification for horrors for which there was certainly a spontaneous taste" and notes that the English translators enlarged on "Seneca's horrors by an inborn taste for loathsome details."[66] Relevant here is Praz's interpretation of Giraldi Cinthio, a 16th-century Italian imitator of Seneca who provided a theory of maximized violence. He revised Aristotle's theory of tragedy in such a way as to legitimize more horror. Thus, instead of being relaxed by the experience of catharsis, the spectator felt "astonishment and 'a thrill which puts the spectator beside himself.' "[67] We will discuss the present state of catharsis theory later, but for now the point is to present shock and astonishment as elements of appeal in popular entertainment.

It is not my intention to suggest a long-range Senecan influence on 20th-century popular art. However, as the writer celebrated above other classical dramatists for the detailing of violent effects, his example is relevant. For instance, *Thyestes* depends on two levels of shock, as E. F. Watling points out: "the horror-climax of the murders (described) and the banquet (enacted)"[68]; he notes also a difference in the formal distribution of violence between Seneca and his Elizabethan imitators: "In Seneca the atrocity is the end and climax to which the whole play points, in the Elizabethan tragedy-chronicle it is . . . to be expected anywhere, at the beginning, middle, or end of the story."[69]

Top and bottom, *Man Without a Star,* Universal Pictures.

The American cinema has many films of both types, but with a significant preponderance of the allover distribution of violence. There is also a combinatory form in which one gun duel has a particular climactic importance, but the route to it is a succession of shocks and killings, as in *Seven Men from Now*. It is in terms of a non-cathartic excitement, therefore, that Senecan and Elizabethan tragedy can be related to the film of violence. As Praz observed: "the audience of an Elizabethan theatre must not have been very different from a modern cinema audience; they cared chiefly for the spectacular and the sensational."[70]

Obviously popular heroes are expected to operate in extreme situations, what technologists call "threshold, or outer limit, testing." The question is, then, what is a man's breaking point, in what areas can a hero be defeated, or, conversely, at what point will a pacific hero be provoked? This is the meaning of the theme of the provoked and persecuted man that runs through an immense number of Westerns *(The Last Wagon,* 1957, is a good example) and crime films *(D.O.A.* is probably the oddest). The battered hero is an inter-genre figure. It should be realized that these up-tight, unshaven men are the typical replacement of the composed and relatively unharmed heroes of earlier movie lore. If this is understood, it can be seen that emphasis is no less on the vulnerability of the hero than on the brutality of the action. Though he is central, though the film is almost certainly seen from the hero's point of view, his actions no longer have an ideal separation from the cause and effect of the world. On the contrary, the hero has ceased to be immune to the violence, as he was in earlier movie conventions. Violence in the American movie is one of the signs of humanity in genres that, without violence, tend to be merely fantastic or primitive. The Western landscape, which has always been Darwinian, is represented now in its full menace. It is inhabited by men who are, in an existentialist sense, thrown into the world, and their "struggle for survival" is no longer shielded by euphemy or discretion.

Recently the enumeration of deaths and the specifics of injury in movies have increased in terms of shock and surprise. Italian Westerns were the immediate cause of this increase in the blood count, and their success produced American imitators. The history of the Western since World War II, however, leads logically to the present level of violence. In the early 50s there was a group of films expressly devoted to studying the power that new weapons gave their owners in the late 19th century and to the social impact of new weapons. These films included *Winchester 73* and *Colt 45,* both 1950, *Only the Valiant,* 1951 (Gatling gun), *Battle of Apache Pass,* 1952 (cannon), and *The Siege of Red River,* 1954 (Gatling gun). They were accompanied by a general increase in precision about weapons, as in *Across the Wide Missouri,* 1951, where the outcome of the final fight hangs on the speed with which the hero can reload his single-shot rifle as an Indian with a tomahawk charges toward him. The cycle of weapon Westerns continued in the middle and late 50s but with a shift from technology to operational lore and responsibility. Without any loss of technical precision, guns were set into a moral framework of right and wrong usage. Some films of this cycle are *Man Without a Star,* 1955, *The Young Guns,* 1956, *The Tin Star,* 1957, *Gunman's Walk* and *Saddle the Wind,* both 1958. Partly this technical stress can be ascribed to the effect in audiences of veterans who had handled guns in World War II and in Korea, but the cold-war discussions of the period about arms standardization for the NATO forces may also have contributed.

One of the most significant developments in recent Westerns is the increased visibility of wounds. The level of information that is available in the other media is bound to have its analogues in the topical medium of film. For instance, it is reported that Vietnam casualties, for all the speed and caliber of medical care, have more severe injuries in some respects than soldiers in earlier wars. These have two main causes, high-velocity rifle bullets that cause massive destruction and mortar or rocket shells which produce extensive multiple wounds. Westerns of the second half of the 50s have responded to developments of modern weapon technology, even when the guns are Colt 45s and Winchester 73s. The impact of bullets from these guns had been persistently understated in past films and now it is being, if anything, overstated. One of the first feature films to specify impact and wounds with a new abundance of blood was *Party Girl,* 1958, a film set in Chicago in the 30s with numerous gang killings.

The calibration of death in popular culture can be paralleled by this quotation from an army technical manual describing the symptoms of nerve-gas poisoning: "running nose, tightness of chest, dimness of vision, pinpointing of eye pupils, difficulty in breathing, drooling, excessive sweating, nausea, vomiting, cramps, involuntary defecation and urination, twitching, jerking, staggering, headache, confusion, drowsiness, coma, convulsion, cessation of breathing, death."[71]

Kiss Me Deadly, United Artists Corp.

Iconography

Mr. Beaser: In other words, when NBC offered *Borderland* to the stations it did contain scenes of Hopalong Cassidy bleeding to death?
Mr. Heffernan: I would doubt Hopalong Cassidy bleeding to death, because the man never dies.
Mr. Beaser: It looked like he was bleeding to death.
Mr. Heffernan: It may have looked like he was bleeding.
Testimony of Joseph V. Heffernan, Vice President, National Broadcasting Co., Inc., New York. Herbert Wilton Beaser, Chief Counsel. *Hearings Before the Subcommittee to Investigate Juvenile Delinquency of the Committee of the Judiciary, United States Senate, 83rd Congress, 2nd session, June 5, October 19 and 20, 1954* (Washington, D.C.: U.S. Government Publication #4562, 1955).

The cinema's persistent technological changes have all been in the direction of more efficient illusion, but these changes are countered by the fact that movies are also highly conservative. In response to the competition of television, cinema screens expanded laterally, presented higher definition of detail, and with the aid of special glasses the image became sculpturesque. At the same time earlier film successes were remade with the new gear so that the novelties of increased illusionism, with an immense amount of new activity in the visual field, were balanced by the peaceful resurgence of known material. Primitive story lines were persuasively restyled. A recent case of efficient illusion blended with archaic content is *2001: A Space Odyssey*, 1968, in which a script that is basically no more complex than Georges Méliès's *A Trip to the Moon*, 1902, is stretched to super-length by luxurious *trompe l'oeil*. Another use of static, ready-made expressive elements in combination with technical innovation was the group of horror movies made by Hammer Studios, England, in the late 50s. Here the Frankenstein monster, Count Dracula, and the Mummy, celebrated from ragged prints on small black-and-white screens, were seen in big-screen color for the first time. (Roger Corman's *new* horror stories in 'Scope and color that followed were a logical next step.) These are extreme cases of a persistent problem for film-makers: the alignment of novel and conservative factors in movies. Reconciling these contraries leads to the happy fulfillment of expectation combined with the sting of surprise and wonder. Probably the best way to discuss the recurrent sustaining factors is by iconographical analysis.

To quote Panofsky: "Iconography is that branch of the history of art which concerns itself with the subject matter or meaning of works of art, as opposed to their form."[72] Though he is closely identified with the subject of iconography in his art-historical writings, he did not attach much importance to it in the movies. He brilliantly defined the terms of the reality of the photographed image but was less attentive to the possibilities of a popular, adaptive iconography. He referred to the survival "quite legitimate, I think—of the remnants of a 'fixed attitude and attribute' principle and, more basic, a primitive and folkloristic concept of plot construction."[73] This is true, but at the date he wrote, 1934, his examples of movie iconography were overweighted in the direction of earlier stereotypes. He instanced the role of the butler in mysteries and a baby's sickness as the solution of "matrimonial problems."

The examples Panofsky cited do not really do justice to the scope and flexibility of movie iconography but imply a simpler situation than really exists. Iconographical analysis depends on the "knowledge of literary sources (familiarity with specific themes and concepts)."[74] In the movies the pursuit of the expression of "themes or concepts ... by objects and events"[75] is slightly different. There is no prior body of literature that provides one-to-one clues as to subject matter, though there are some useful literary sources. To identify iconographical continuities in the movies, it is necessary to derive the information from adequate samples of the films themselves. That is why I have been obliged to cite so many films in the course of this essay. Several preexisting categories of films exist traditionally, however, and provide a convenient starting point. Classification by genres (genus, kind, sort, style) is applicable because both Hollywood and its audience recognize such groupings as the Western, horror film, war film, soap opera, gangster, and prison film. Let us consider some of these preexisting types as a preliminary iconographical grouping. In this way we can indicate typical patterns of recurrence and change in popular films which can be traced better in terms of iconography than in terms of individual creativity. Indeed, the personal contribution of many directors can only be seen fully after typical iconographical elements have been identified.

Take the gangster film; in the 30s such films, especially those made by Warner Brothers, echoed the headlines of the late 20s and 30s. The impact of these sharp and capable movies, close behind the actual events, was considerable. Robert Warshow nominated two of the cycle, *Little Caesar*, 1930, and *Scarface*, 1932, as "archetypal gangster movies."[76] It follows from this, as Warshow stated, that "the gangster movie . . . no longer exists in its 'classical' form."[77] That his view has some currency is shown by the celebrity that still clings to *early* Edward G. Robinson, *early* Paul Muni, *early* James Cagney. Warshow wrote in 1954, almost ten years after a postwar revival of the genre which he ignored. *White Heat,* with Cagney, is a significant film of the type, as was *The Enforcer,* 1951, the first film to use congressional committee reports about the nationwide organization of crime. It began a series of syndicate-crime movies (the British title of the film was, significantly, *Murder Incorporated),* which carry on and modify the form of gangster films which developed in the 30s.

The gangster has never been, as the villain of a Western can be, a dark and savage side of the hero, the Cain in every Abel. The gangster tends to function as a dark side of big business, the negative image of the entrepreneur as hero. As such he is identified with uncontrollable events in the city rather than with individual reaction to changing events. We watch gangster films as if they were morality plays; that is to say, we wait for the abstract distribution of penalties and deaths, which, given our prior knowledge of the genre and of the then-working Production Code, are predictable. There is a detachment in watching gangster films, inasmuch as the characters are always visibly progressing to their deaths. The main question is: who will they take with them? Unlike the intimacy we feel with Western heroes, there is a strong element of alienation, though it takes different forms in prewar and postwar films. *Public Enemy,* 1931, for instance, was a rags-to-riches success story set in the rackets instead of legitimate business. In *Al Capone,* 1956, the gangster goes from being "a boy with a future" to becoming "Mr. Big." The biographical form is used in both films, but the business-career aspect is stressed far more than the ethic of individual effort in the later one. The dialogue of *Al Capone* makes it clear that gangsters are not in crime for symptomatic or pathological reasons. They would abhor the idea of crime as anarchy on which Fritz Lang's Dr. Mabuse films were based. Capone says, "I'm not a gangster. I'm a businessman. 'Serve the public,' that's my motto."

The gangster film of the mid-50s, for all its traditional slaughter, concentrates on crime at the level of decision-making. In *Al Capone* the first meetings are like disputes between Italians who might be running a restaurant; then, with prosperity, the film shades into executive meetings in a board room with Gothic windows. Thus the emphasis is on crime as business, which changes considerably the image of the 30s, the period in which the film is set, from the gangster films made at the time. Obviously this is different from the supposed archetypal pattern, but why not? In *White Heat,* Cagney plays a gangster, as he had in *Public Enemy,* but instead of being a figure explainable by naturalistic sociology, as in the 30s film, he is a tormented man with an oedipal attachment to his mother, prone to migraine and convulsions (affective epilepsy?). He is abhorrent in his violence, but the hero, a T-man, is contaminated when he wins the gangster's confidence only for the purpose of betraying him. The hero is, as it were, a good Judas—a situation repeated in a later film, *House of Bamboo,* which crossed the gangster genre with wide-screen tourism set in Japan. In *House of Bamboo* the moral paradox is made explicit when the gangster invokes Cain, though in an obscure way, by asking "Am I my brother's keeper?" after saving the life of the hero who will later destroy him. There is a sophistication concerning institutions and relationships that amplifies the gangster film without destroying the genre. Thus for Warshow to enforce a cutoff point in the development of such films, by making a past phase canonical, is premature and obstructive. The genre continued after the war, sporadic but reliable, sometimes appearing in a pure form, as in *The St. Valentine's Day Massacre,* 1967, sometimes blurring into police-investigation films, such as *The Case Against Brooklyn,* 1958.

The ambiguous role of the hero as he penetrates criminal groups is often accompanied by ritual degradation; as he simulates criminality he sacrifices the forms of his earlier life. These hidden heroes hold virtue and deception in suspense in a curious mix of corrective zeal and sneaky inside knowledge. In one sense such deceptions can be linked to the traditional theme of the false heir, usually a substitute for a long-lost son identifiable by the attribute of a birthmark, a locket, or an item of family knowledge. (A late example of this motif is *Branded,* 1950, an Alan Ladd Western.) The motif of clandestine investigation, in which the hero is right but morally suspect, has a current-affairs content that supplements the folklore. After World War II the investigations of undercover agents became the most publicized of secret activities. *I Was a Communist for the FBI,* 1951, is an early example of the genre, though not one of the best, and its release coincided with an FBI undercover agent's memoirs, the best-selling *I Led Three Lives.* Since then the FBI, in extensively reported cases, has infiltrated the Ku Klux Klan, the Mafia, and the Minutemen, exposed corruption in New York City government, and most recently penetrated protest organizations. Linked to these burrowing actions is the use of electronic techniques of surveillance. *Touch of Evil,* 1958, which is all about the definition of justice, is resolved by the villain's self-incrimination via an electronic bug, a technique still under discussion by the Supreme Court. *White Heat* and *House of Bamboo* combine both the duplicity of the hero and the use of up-to-date radio equipment. *The Case Against Brooklyn* and *The Scarface Mob,* 1962, both indicate technical problems of wiretapping, such technological detail being typical of many crime films.

American democracy has a traditional abhorrence of both informing and eavesdropping and certainly their paralleling the techniques of secret police in totalitarian countries is disturbing. The participation of heroes in this contested area of criminal rights is typical of the complexity of postwar popular culture. These situations exceed the constraints of liberal opinion, but the presentation of the problems in a hard-nosed way does not constitute their endorsement. It does, however, situate the hero in a world without simple values, and this is, I take it, a naturalistic view of events.

Prison films, a minor but legible group, have changed significantly since the 30s, when, as in *You Only Live Once,* 1937, prison was an episode in a criminal's biography, part of an underworld rake's progress. The shift of meaning is traceable to the influence of the reports and memoirs of prisoners of war after World War II. Within this context, prison became linked with problems of liberty as part of a body of popular existentialism. A characteristic film is *Brute Force,* in which the escape, planned by a convict with an army background, ends in death for all. To ensure that we get the idea that the prison is a symbol of all institutions, the prison doctor, a drunken Greek chorus, asks, "Why do they try? Nobody escapes. Nobody ever escapes." The prisoner of war literature, when not committed to the record of atrocity, provided studies of behavior and status within a closed system. Societies appear everywhere, and the camp, like prison, was an analogue of the world outside rather than an arena of deprivation and torture. On this basis it was even possible to make P.O.W. comedies *(Stalag 17,* 1953, was the first, following prison comedies like *My Six Convicts,* 1952).

Examples of connections within the field of mass communications, the linking of one channel to another, such as the influence of P.O.W. memoirs, can be multiplied. It is worth doing so, because such correspondences have been neglected by film critics intent in their search for purely cinematic masterpieces. Instead of concentrating on the supposedly unique features of the medium, we need to consider the crossovers among communicative forms. Only then can we chart the forms that topicality takes in movies, often oblique but definitely present as a predisposing factor in the audience's attitudes. Let us take the private-detective movie and discuss it in relation to its literary origin.

The film that effectively popularized the private-eye genre was John Huston's *The Maltese Falcon,* an almost literal transcription of Dashiel Hammett's novel. This genre prospered briefly between the two phases of gangster film already discussed. Here is Raymond Chandler's account of the genesis of his first book: *"The Big Sleep* was written in the spring of 1938 [published 1939] and was based on two novelettes called *Killer in the Rain,* published January 1935, and *The Curtain,* published September 1936. Included in this book also was a fairly long sequence taken from a novelette called *The Man Who Liked Dogs,* published March 1936."[78] Here is a clear statement of the novel's origin in pulp fiction (so called for the thick and shaggy wood-pulp paper on which the magazines were printed) which in the years between the wars succeeded the dime novels and weekly story magazines of the 19th and early 20th centuries. In the 30s there were as many as two hundred of these magazines, including *Black Mask,* which developed the American private-detective story as an alternative of the polite British puzzle story, or its American adaptations, such as those of S.S. Van Dine.[79]

The plotting of private-detective films is complicated, sometimes obscure. Chandler has recorded his version of a variously repeated story that goes like this: "When Howard Hawks was making *The Big Sleep,* the movie, he and Bogart got into an argument as to whether one of the characters was murdered or committed suicide. They sent a wire asking me, and dammit I didn't know either."[80] Puzzles in detective fiction are always pseudo-puzzles, the simulated precision of which can be resolved in various ways until the last moment. Chandler recorded, too, that "I hate explanation scenes and I learned in Hollywood that there are two rules about them. (1) You can give only a little at a time, if there is much to give. (2) You can only have an explanation when there is some other element, such as danger or love-making, or a character reversal expected."[81] Hawks and his writer William Faulkner adapted *The Big Sleep,* 1946, fairly roughly, cutting short a series of revelations so that a girl would not turn out to be the killer. The form of the private-eye story as Chandler, not Hammett, developed it is molecular, with connections and ramifications across society counting for more than fair clues in closed rooms. As the movies adapted the form, it meant that the audience was freed from causal narrative to a greater extent than in the novels, where you can check back; in the films one is precipitated into a series of episodes. This relaxation of tight continuity is another example of the principle of approximate coherence already mentioned.

Chandler, like Hammett, took stories written for the pulps and expanded them to novel length, but in addition, Chandler unified the episodic form by the mood of his narrator. He created a tough and literate narrator, sweet and sour, at the center of action and betrayal. This is what the feature films with private-detective subjects also did, filling out the central character with a dogged humanity. Other actors played private eyes, such as Dick Powell in *Murder, My Sweet,* 1945, and Mark Stevens in *Dark Corner,* but Humphrey Bogart dominates the genre, playing both Sam Spade in *The Maltese Falcon* and Philip Marlowe in *The Big Sleep.*

Chandler's Marlowe, like Ross Macdonald's later detective Lew Archer, is a great moralist, forever extending or withholding compassion, larding irony with anger or understanding, bracing sympathy with scathing judgment or therapeutic iron. When Mickey Spillane's *Kiss Me Deadly* was filmed in 1955, the Chandleresque tradition was sufficiently strong to transform even Mike Hammer's barbarism. The vanity, resentment, and brutality of Spillane's first-person narrative were shifted, so that the urban milieu became mysterious rather than incoherent. Corruption is used by Spillane as justification for his hero's savagery, as if a truck driver's beating up of a homosexual were to be regarded as a moral judgment. Corruption in the Chandleresque genre cannot be so complacently punished. The violence in the movie of *Kiss Me Deadly* is geared to provocation with a more realistic indirection than in the original; here is a case, and there are others, where the Production Code guide lines against excessive violence pushed a movie toward subtlety. Suspense (that is, nothing happening) and moodiness are as real in the film as the brisk sequences of interrogation and fighting. In addition, the mysterious object that everybody is trying to find is significantly altered; in the book it is a box of drugs, and in the film it is a radioactive isotope that destroys the woman who opens the box. This ending is cued by the book, inasmuch as

this character has a horribly scarred body, the result of an unexplained fire before the story begins. By burning her in the film and by burning up the house as well, so potent is the isotope, an undercurrent of Pandora's box is introduced as a deliberately evocative device.

In the 40s and 50s the private eye, as an American vernacular hero of considerable subtlety, was a popular type. The nocturnal milieu and complex plots seem to have been congenial at the time. Crime films from 1948 to 1959 were persistently urban and violent, as is shown by the following titles: *Naked City, Cry of the City, Street with No Name, Panic in the Streets, Mystery Street, Night and the City, Dark City, Where the Sidewalk Ends, Captive City, While the City Sleeps, Slaughter on 10th Avenue,* and *City of Fear.* Does the private eye match the style and folklore of the 60s? Frank Tashlin explained that he did not care for the "basic idea" of his Jerry Lewis movie *It's Only Money,* "Here we are in 1962 doing private eyes."[82] His caustic comment seems accurate in the light of several attempts to revive the form recently: Paul Newman in *Harper,* 1966 taken from Ross Macdonald's *The Moving Target;* Frank Sinatra in *Tony Rome,* 1967, and its sequel of the following year, *Lady in Cement;* Kirk Douglas in *A Lovely Way to Die,* 1968. *Harper* ends inconclusively with the hero's moral problem tossed away; and the Sinatra films, set in Miami, though solidly made, have a period look like those 'Scope films of the mid-50s when the camera was mobile, both on a crane and on location in sunny places. The more permissive sexual code (admitting lesbians and navels, for instance) updates the films mildly, like a five-degree lift in a Cadillac's tail fins, but there is no sense now of the narrative conviction and emotional identification that the early private-eye films could simultaneously assume and create.

When the private eye was king, various writers overanalyzed this type of hero, proposing mythic patterns, usually to do with knights and the grail. It seems more relevant, however, to trace the outward form of this hero from the pulps, through novels, into the movies. There is an objective difficulty about presenting mystery on the screen: the absence of the criminal or doubt about his identity, entertaining in literary whodunits, has not thrived in movies. Gangster films and investigations of known criminals seem more amenable to physical enactment. The puzzle element was at a minimum in private-eye films or at any rate was secondary to the present spectacle of luxurious apartments, sudden fights, ambiguous girls, and insomniac stress.

The theme of corrupt cities, with an emotional topography of dark alleys, shiny cars, shadowed bars, high skylines, and penthouse terraces, characterizes the period. Sometimes the scene is generalized, as in *The Big Heat,* 1953, sometimes specific and quasi-documentary, as in *The Phenix City Story,* which begins with a documentary coverage of the city including interviews with the inhabitants; then there is a studio sequence in which a girl in a bar sings about the sinful city; and finally the actors move into the real locations. In *The Case Against Brooklyn,* there is none of this play on levels of reality, though both films characterize corrupt communities and recount their violent reform. The former film is about a citizens' crusade and the latter about an undercover policeman, an ambitious career cop who is willing to take on another identity if it will lead him to the men behind the rackets. He wins, but he loses (another non-upbeat victory). His best friend is shot; his wife is killed by a bomb meant for him, as in *The Big Heat;* his assumed identity so overrides friendship and love that he finally rejects even the woman he courted in his assumed identity. "It's a great day—for Brooklyn," the police commissioner tells the hero, hospitalized with gunshot wounds. In *Man in the Shadow,* 1957, a group of citizens warns the local sheriff who is investigating a millionaire rancher that he is killing their town. "This isn't a town, it's a trained dog act," snaps the hero. For all the faith in democracy that French critics have seen symbolized in the libertarian panning shots in American movies, the scripts and situations are repeatedly skeptical of communities and anti-populist in their characterization of groups.

Parallel to the private-detective and corrupt-city themes is the problem film of the late 40s. What is important in these films from our point of view is the association of violence with increasingly serious causes. Consider two treatments of anti-Semitism, both of 1947: one, *Gentleman's Agreement,* treats the subject in terms of a soap opera about career, the other, *Crossfire,* in terms of a murder mystery culminating with the killer's being shot down in the street. A good many films of this cycle are vulnerable to sophisticated criticism of their evasions as *tracts,* but from the standpoint of violent movies their value is considerable, because social problems and issues are presented in terms of vivid action. As a result, the capacity of violent movies to deal with situations less tranquilizing than the drama of earlier days was enhanced. Two of the movies of 1947 with documentary locations and scripts based on fact, *Boomerang* and *Call Northside 777,* deal with judicial error. In *Knock on Any Door,* 1949, juvenile delinquency is the problem and in *No Way Out,* 1950, racial prejudice; Bogart in the former as a crusading attorney, Widmark in the latter as a psychopathic racist, ensure by their presence the intensity of crime films within the public-affairs content. *He Walked by Night,* 1949, and *The Sniper,* 1950, are studies of psychopaths with rifles, and in both cases it is their solitude as much as the pressures of the chase that is brought out. Delinquency was the subject of *Rebel Without a Cause, Blackboard Jungle, Mad at the World,* all 1955, and *Crime in the Streets,* 1956. In all these films violence is not the athletics of an adventure film but the emblematic expression of current tensions.

The conspicuous role of the male in films of violence should not obscure the persistence of a traditional feminine type. The iconography of the 19th-century *femme fatale* has been documented by Mario Praz.[83] Leonardo's *La Gioconda,* interpreted in terms of a strange fatality by Walter Pater, is part of it: "the unfathomable smile, always with a touch of something sinister in it. . . . Hers is the head upon which all 'the ends of the world are come,' and the eyelids are a little weary. . . . Set it for a moment beside one of those white Greek goddesses or beautiful women of antiquity, and how would they be troubled by this beauty, into which the soul with all its maladies has passed!"[84] In this form the *femme fatale* appeared in the early cinema (Theda Bara's name is an anagram for Arab Death, incidentally). After the *femme fatale,* whose background includes Salome and Judith, we might anglicize her later transformations as simply "fatal woman." In the 40s she was a frequent type in movies derived from private-detective stories: both *The Maltese Falcon* and *Murder, My Sweet* eventually nominate the central female character as the killer. One of the most elaborate appearances of the fatal woman is to be found in *The Lady from Shanghai;* when the hero and the woman meet, they swap the names of far away, mostly "wicked," places where she was born and had worked but which the hero has merely visited as a sailor. As a lady from Shanghai, she speaks a Chinese dialect that helps her in the final chase after the hero in San Francisco's Chinatown. The worldliness and malaise of the fatal woman appear here in terms of a restless itinerary and exceptional linguistic powers.

Rita Hayworth is the center of the action, as of the hero's attention; she is corrupt, but her motives are less clear than the fact of her guilt. This failure to motivate her character clearly does the film no harm at all; she remains the glamorous cause of a

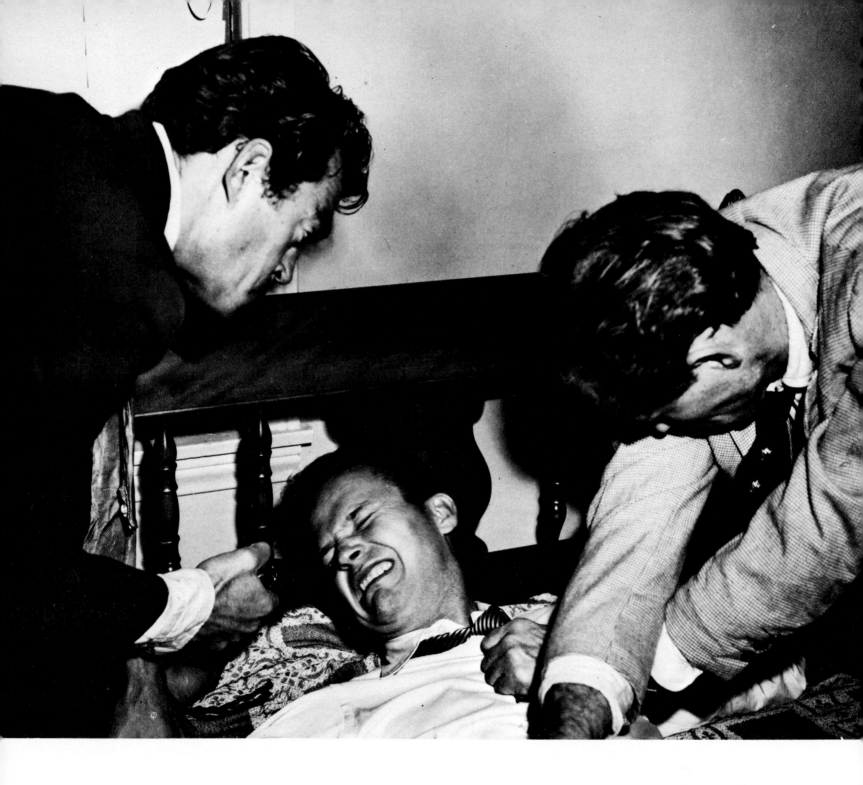

Kiss Me Deadly, United Artists Corp.

The Big Heat, Columbia Pictures Corp.

Top, *Touch of Evil,* Universal Pictures.
Bottom, *The Big Heat,* Columbia Pictures Corp.

Top, *The Killers,* 1964, Universal Pictures.
Bottom, *The Case Against Brooklyn,* Columbia Pictures Corp.

49

narrative in which explanations are fragmented over different sequences. In other movies of the time, like the 1946 version of *The Killers* or *Out of the Past,* 1947, there is a similar concentration on obscurely motivated but physically irresistible women. They are not explainable, as is for instance the Marlene Dietrich character in *Der Blaue Engel (The Blue Angel),* 1930, in terms of a Strindbergian malevolent biology. Full explanations are withheld, but the attributes are clear: intricate patterns of double cross and sexual mobility. These women seem prompted as much by drifting as by greed, as much by doubt as by ambition. That Ava Gardner turns out to be behind the tangled plot of *The Killers* enhances her centrality, which is more important than equipping her with purposes. (Her later films like *Pandora and the Flying Dutchman,* 1951, and *The Barefoot Contessa,* 1954, amplified this role.)

In *Ramrod,* the heroine, Veronica Lake, as we know right along but the hero does not, precipitates all the trouble, the deaths. (In *Man Without a Star,* another Western, the trouble begins with a woman, too, but she is fully explained as bossy and ambitious.) By the mid-50s, the time of *Kiss Me Deadly,* ultimate guilt is expected to be located in a woman. In *Out of the Past,* Jane Greer swings between two men, played by Robert Mitchum and Kirk Douglas, who engage in intricate competition, but the reference point of real evil remains the Jane Greer character. When *The Killers* was originally adapted for the screen, Anthony Veiller took the Ernest Hemingway short story, kept it intact for the opening sequence, and made the rest of the film an explanation of the assassination: it is an intricate choreography of deceptions around Ava Gardner. When it was remade in 1964, the Veiller elaborations were preserved in outline, but the new director, Don Siegel, is on record as saying: "The character of Angie Dickinson was not only dishonest, it was badly written. I was never able to make the part make sense."[85] It is true that fatal women are no longer current as mysterious presences as in the 40s, but it matters little that Angie Dickinson's character is not individually motivated. As an iconographical type she does not need to be supplied with a seething unconscious mind of her own nor a cache of reasonable self-interest on which to draw. Once she is recognized as a set figure, she has a functional role; she explains the plot and does not herself need explaining psychologically. The fatal woman is defined by the hero's torment; she is there to appear unexpectedly-expected with an older man—Albert Dekker in the first version, Ronald Reagan in the remake.

There are links between the period when fatal women were easily their own self-justification and Siegal's naturalistic doubts. There are the Ava Gardner location dramas already mentioned and related characters like the girl played by Cyd Charisse in *Two Weeks in Another Town,* 1962. As a long-legged, confident, promiscuous jet-set girl, she is not explained in terms of psychology, but she is formulaically smooth to everybody who knows the convention. Thus the meaning is carried more by the iconographical significance of the part than by depth of individual characterization.

Owing to the compound nature of films, there are both space and time for allusions which might be regarded as the mythical aspect of the movies. In *White Heat* a robbery is being discussed with the gangsters planning to enter a factory by hiding inside a truck; explaining the plan, James Cagney refers to an old wooden horse. This classical reference is overt, whereas in *Kiss Me Deadly* the myth of Pandora is implicit. In the early version of *The Killers* there is allusion of another kind: one of the characters in the sequence taken straight from the Hemingway story is called Nick Adams, a name the author used in autobiographical stories. You do not have to get the allusion for the sequence to work, but the reference is a neat one, putting a symbol of the author into his own work as a witness.

The movie *El Dorado,* 1967, is taken from a novel by Harry Brown, *The Stars in Their Courses,* which is a repeat of events in the Iliad, laboriously rationalized as events in the 19th-century West. When Leigh Brackett adapted the novel for Howard Hawks she abandoned the cyclic myth (history repeating itself). If there is anything mythic about the film, it would have to arise from the situations such as one man's redeeming another from drink; a young man, half son, half mascot, who follows an older man; and the clash of two gunfighters committed to opposing sides but keeping in professional contact. The problem is: because such figures are heroic in scale, can they be called mythical? Does their iconographical form really entail elevation to the status of myth?

To answer this question we must define myth more strictly than is usual in film criticism. A myth is a narrative concerning divine beings, the origins of which may lie in the cycles of nature—agricultural or celestial—in primary family relationships, or in cultural change. The affect of a myth derives from its closeness to basic human and social experience and from its broad acceptance by a community. Mythology necessarily consists of an array of stand-

The Killers, 1964, Universal Pictures.

Top, *The Killers*, 1946, Universal Pictures.
Bottom, *I Walk Alone*, Paramount Pictures Corp.

ardized interpretations; without a prescribed meaning we are not dealing with myth. There was a strong movement in the first half of the 20th century to formulate continuities between ancient myths and the present by means of recurrent situations or reborn heroes. This is the period of Hamlet as Oedipus, London as a wasteland, Dublin as the site of the Odyssey; constant historical patterns are proposed as absolutes. It was done by Ernest Jones in psychoanalysis, by T. S. Eliot in poetry, and by James Joyce in the novel, and all of them rely on literary allusions that readers can be trained to recognize. This mythology represents an agreed–on body of knowledge, though purely literary.

The situation at the movies cannot be satisfactorily explained as either an original mythical experience or as derivative of earlier myths. In the absence of any broadly shared cosmology, summed up in a public genealogy of relationships and pinpointed by a chart of easily accessible attributes and functions, mythology amounts to very little. It is not an atmosphere. Myth is a "legendary story, usually concerning some superhuman being or some alleged person or event, with or without a determinable basis of fact or a natural explanation, especially a traditional or legendary story that is concerned with deities or demigods and the creation of the world." Myth is also "any invented story, or concept." What is meant by myth at the movies is usually only the latter vulgar meaning, not the first grandiose sense. Idealized characters and stereotyped plots are called mythological when in fact they are simply iconographical. E. R. Curtius has put another argument against over-mythicization very well in another context: "The fabulatory function has risen from producing fiction for biological ends to creating gods and myths, and has finally freed itself entirely from the world of religion to become a free play."[86] The wonders of movies are the marvels of show business, and the heroes are the condensations of topical interests rather than the recurrence of ancient mysteries.

The movies generate a great deal of fantastic imagery but more in relation to present needs than according to timeless patterns. The adaptive forms rather than the archaic origins of myth are expressive. The movies confer grandeur on the present by dealing with current events in maximal forms. Hollywood's preoccupation with heroes must obviously include some mythical analogies, but it is important not to go from this objective resemblance to a view of the movies as one great mirror of conservative fantasy, a Jungian screening room of old favorites. In fact, the fantastic is often better regarded separately from mythology, despite the conflation of the two by psychoanalysts and surrealists.

Consider the evocative situations of two violent movies, The Man with My Face, 1951, and D.O.A. In the former the hero is displaced from his home and framed for robbery by a double who is accepted by his wife. In D.O.A. the hero, for no reason known to himself or to the audience, is poisoned fairly early in the film by a slow-acting but fatal shot of a radioactive substance. The rest of the film is his walking, running, searching to make sense of his death. In The Man with My Face there is a comparable frantic quest, this time in search of identity. Both films establish a paranoid sense of the hostile and unreliable environment. True, there is an allusive hint of misgivings about doppelgängers in one and a kind of "memoirs of a reluctant sacrifice" in the other, but basically the films are not about unconscious fears or archaic patterns. They are part of popular culture's equivalent of the literature of extreme situations that came out of the political persecutions of the 30s and World War II.

One of the dangers of genre theory is that the categories may be taken rigidly. When that happens they lose their descriptive usefulness and assume a normative function. An example of the desire for stability is Robert Warshow's "The Westerner," an article first published in 1954. As in his text on gangster movies he looks back to locate a classical point from which to judge the whole genre. "The Western hero . . ." he writes, "is a figure in repose" and "not thus compelled to seek love. . . .[87] Warshow's archetypal Western is The Virginian, based on Owen Wister's novel of 1902, as it was made in 1929 with Gary Cooper. Warshow's aim is to freeze the Western at an early point of stylized morality. Whereas the private-detective movies derived from a new style of story originated in popular magazines of the 20s and 30s, Warshow's perfect Western derives from the archaic pattern of late-19th-century popular fiction.

A sociologist, more observant than nostalgic, has indicated the real situation. Joseph Klapper, referring to an article by Frederick Elkin written in 1950, writes "Elkin performed a qualitative analysis of old-style Western movies, many of which are, of course, current television fare. Justice, he found, always prevailed. The typical hero of the time neither smoke nor drank, did not lose his temper, fought fair, and was a paragon of democratic social attitudes."[88] While admitting Elkin's observations, Klapper goes on to examine the changing situation: "Virtually all of the cited analyses bear upon media material of five or more years ago and cannot automatically be assumed to be wholly valid in reference to current offerings. The hero of the currently popular 'adult Western,' for example, is most unlike the Galahads observed by Elkin; today's hero may smoke, often holds his liquor better than does the villain, and is frequently more neurotic than democratic."[89] All varieties of Westerns are still being made either by the movies or by television. Thus Warshow's myth can at best be said to apply to a group of Westerns made at one time. The genre as a whole, however, needs to be approached in a way that can accommodate change.

It is essential to treat the popular arts as a process in time and not to arrest the succession in quest of masterpieces. Genres are useful as a descriptive technique only if we define runs or sets, not isolated works. Rather as the modern Western presents the world in Darwinian terms (one group is always displacing another), we need to regard the development of genres in an evolutionary framework. Film critics who regard the Western as timeless and idyllic neglect the fact that films continually focus on individual competition and on social change as subjects. The Western is a Darwinian jungle, not an Edenic garden. Let us trace some characteristic movies that indicate the major changes that took place in the convention as "adult" Westerns supplemented the "kid stuff."

The change in the Western is a postwar phenomenon. In 1947 *Duel in the Sun* was released, an expensive feature film in which the Western was given a massive injection of violence and sensuality. Viewed today, this effort to get the sensationalism of historical novels into the traditional format is coarse. In the same year, *Ramrod* successfully enlarged the pattern of behavior tolerated within the form. The violence is calibrated with a new precision: death by shotgun, protracted death after beating, callous shooting of an old man, and bloody faces after a slow-phased fistfight between heavyweights (McCrea and Lloyd Bridges). In the following year films like *Red River, Yellow Sky,* and *Blood on the Moon* maintained the traditional contour of the Western while transforming it internally: motivations became more tangled, violence more specific, locales more diverse, and fancy dress disappeared. Howard Hawks, therefore, was exaggerating his independence when he said: "When I made *Red River,* I thought an adult western could be made for mature audiences, and now everyone is making 'intelligent' westerns."[90] (Incidentally, this group of Westerns anticipates by several years Warshow's formula, which cannot contain them.)

Broken Arrow, 1950, was among the first of a cycle of anthropological Westerns, encouraged by the recently formed National Film Committee of the Association on Indian Affairs. Good and bad values are evenly distributed among whites and Indians. In *The Devil's Doorway,* 1950, Robert Taylor played an Indian good enough to fight in the War Between the States but victimized by real estate operators on his return home. (Three years later, in *Arrowhead,* the Indians are characterized as mean and savage on an anthropological basis, but this is a rare double take.) John Ford's group of *Fort Apache, She Wore a Yellow Ribbon, Wagonmaster,* and *Rio Grande* was released between 1948 and 1950. Nostalgically phrased as they are, the cumulative effect of these movies, as a saga of the Southwest, helped to raise the Western's prestige and extend its range. In *Wagonmaster,* for example, the characterization as a primal male clan of the Cleggs, who terrorize the wagon train, is very well done, drawing on a new style of acting and on a new sense of criminality as the expression of invincible stupidity. In 1951 Hathaway directed *Rawhide* with Jack Elam as the kind of psychopath that Widmark had played four years earlier in the same director's *Kiss of Death.* Such inter-genre borrowing was made possible by the increasing sophistication of the once-innocent Western.

Themes introduced at this time and extended in the 50s reveal the expanded capacity of the genre, which was the result of aging stars (who needed more complex vehicles), intelligent writers, and conscientious directors, all of whom were supported by an audience that had acquired as a result of war and/or college a knowingness about motivation and violence. After World War I there was a recoil from violence that seems to have had no equivalent in the aftermath of World War II. One form of popular cynicism is worth noting here. The untrustworthiness of the whites is the theme of numerous films, including several hostile characterizations of General Custer, implicitly, in *Fort Apache,* 1948, by name in *Sitting Bull,* 1954. In *Run of the Arrow,* 1957, an elaborate play of Yankee and Southern, white and Indian loyalties, the hero sums up an army officer by saying "the West is full of frustrated Custers." By steps Custer became a symbol for opinionated, by-the-book militarism.

The visual quality of the new Westerns is often marvelous; an intensified sense of space and light in outdoor settings; the alternations of long, patient pans and sudden flickering images of fast-cut gunfights, staged with a new rage and ingenuity. Consider the inhabited landscape of movies like

Top, *Sands of Iwo Jima,* Republic Pictures Corp.
Bottom, *The Steel Helmet,* Lippert Pictures.

Top, *The Left Handed Gun*, Warner Bros. Pictures Corp.
Bottom, *The Last Wagon*, Twentieth Century-Fox Film Corp.

Backlash, 1956, and *The Naked Spur;* every feature of landscape is assessed as a foxhole or vantage point, as an ambush for *us* or for *them.* Thus the visual clarity and elegance of the photography increases the terrain's potential for threat, so that the landscape becomes the analogue of an ever more treacherous cast of characters. For example, *Only the Valiant* is an Indians-versus-the cavalry film, but the army unit is an expendable group of horse thieves, deserters, misfits, and psychopaths who give the hero as much trouble as the attacking Indians. It is worth recording that this cavalry Western, starring Gregory Peck, is a very knowing extension and reworking of *Twelve O'Clock High,* released one year earlier, which is also about the strains of leadership. In the war film Peck brings order to a bomber squadron that has collapsed into a pile of amiable or guilty misfits, and then collapses himself; in the later Western he holds himself together and completes his mission without the weakness revealed in the earlier role.

In a group of James Stewart films, 1950-57 *(Winchester 73, Bend of the River, The Far Country,* all three written by Borden Chase and directed by Anthony Mann, as well as Mann's *Naked Spur* and Chase's *Night Passage)* there are variations on a Cain-and-Abel rivalry between brothers or between men close enough to be brothers. Loyalties are tangled in Westerns, and the reasons for pulling the trigger have now become complex and painful as never before. There are oedipal conflicts and conflicts between brothers. In *Run for Cover,* 1955, and *Gunman's Walk,* a father is forced to accept the fact that his adopted or natural son is a killer. In the latter film the bad son is killed by his father and the last image is a vertical shot of the body filling the 'Scope screen like a coffin. *Backlash* has the most complex oedipal play of all: the hero is searching for the man who betrayed his father by abandoning him in a small group under attack by Indians years earlier. He finds the traitorous survivor finally, and it is his father himself, who then tries to kill his son.

Complexity's simplest form is reversal. In *The Ride Back,* 1957, the deputy is awkward, disliked by children, and unhappily married; his prisoner is sympathetic, gets on well with children, and has no problem with women, but he *is* guilty. In *The Last of the Fast Guns,* 1958, the old-fashioned symbolism was inverted: the hero was dour and wore black; the villain was a cheerful fellow in a bright white shirt (Gilbert Roland, in fact). The best of the postwar Westerns are more intricate than this and have a pinto morality of mottled black and white. *Warlock*

is one of the most elaborately shaded of all and is, incidentally, a model adaptation of a long novel into a solid film. Warlock is a small town caught between old-fashioned violence and emerging civilization; the cowboys who were there first have become hooligans as the town that they made possible expands. For protection the citizens hire a gunman who runs the town, if not for law and order, at least for peace and safety. When Warlock gets a legal deputy he and the gunman are forced, despite mutual regard, into opposition. Because the deputy is a renegade from the cowboys he is distrusted by the townspeople; he therefore represents legality against the community's will, whereas the gunman has their guilty support.

The ambiguous functions of force in the community were explored in various ways following *High Noon,* in which a town fails to back its sheriff. This film was written by Carl Foreman as an allegory of Hollywood's failure to back victims of Senator Joseph McCarthy's anti-Communism, of whom Foreman was one. The explicit political reference was soon lost, but the theme of the guilty town remained topical through the 50s. In *The Man with the Gun,* 1955, a town hires a gunman to clean out troublemakers and then recoils at the violence of the operation. In *The Man from Del Rio,* 1956, there is a similar situation, but the stakes are doubled: the hired gunman is Mexican, so that racial prejudice against him appears once the street is made safe by his gun. In *Johnny Concho* an exploited town finally rebels, which also happens in *Man in the Shadow,* where the Western setting is modern. These guilty communities are iconographically linked to the corrupt city in contemporaneous crime films.

Everybody knows death in the Western as spectacular falls from horses, trees, the walls of the fort. These plunges, dives, and collapses mime mortality and are a protection against the real presence of death. It is specificity of wounds, loss of actors with whom the audience identifies, and the sheer number of the dead that can turn the falls of stunt men into disturbing events. The witty athleticism of stunt men defends the audience from dismay; the shock of life's extinction is overwhelmed by admiration of the gymnastics. However, as the motives of Westerners have become more naturalistic, death has become more a physical fact and less a form of play. The efforts to get the villain's corpse out of the fast-running river by the bounty hunters in *The Naked Spur,* the impact of bullets and their exit on the other side of the body *(One-Eyed Jacks, 1961, Shalako, 1968),* a burning man in the final gunfight in *From Hell to Texas,* 1958, all these details rest on pain as real and on death as fact.

The title *Seven Men from Now* refers to the number of men hunted by the hero Randolph Scott, who wants revenge on them for shooting his wife in a robbery. (Scott's *Ride Lonesome,* 1959, is also motivated by a murdered wife, as are *The Last Wagon, Last Train from Gun Hill,* 1959, and *One Foot in Hell,* 1960.) Scott catches up with the first two as the movie opens in the rain—always a sign of realism in a Western; later in a fight among sunny rocks he shoots two more in the head. Adding other people's violence, nine people are killed, including a back shooting, before Scott has cleared the world of his guilty. Counting by deaths is a harsh invention that implicates the spectator by inviting one to keep tally. Boetticher, Kennedy, and Scott made *Seven Men from Now* as well as *The Tall T,* also based on death and the readiness to kill. In the latter, three killers and three captives share a journey, knowing that only one group can expect to survive: a schedule to kill the captives exists from the moment they are taken. There is no compromise that will allow the use of euphemisms such as being "knocked out" or "tied up"; nor is escape possible, as everybody concerned is too professional. When the climax is reached it is symmetrical as well as violent. Early in the film the killers dump three bodies into a well. At the end two of them are dead in a cave as the third, dying from a shotgun blast in the face, rushes blindly into the cave and out again before falling. The opened earth (well or cave) receives the dead, a consignment which the structure of the film forces us to anticipate.

Marshall McLuhan's opinions on the relationship of movies and television are incredible but worth disputing owing to his temporary eminence as a theorist of the mass media. "The movie Western . . . has always been a lowly form. With television, the Western acquired new importance, since its theme is always [sic] 'let's make a town.' "[91] "Moreover, the television image takes kindly to the varied and rough textures of Western saddles, clothes, hides, and shoddy match-wood bars and hotel lobbies. The movie camera, by contrast, is at home in the slick chrome world of the night club and the luxury spots of a metropolis."[92] In fact, of course, the big screens and the depth of focus characteristic of postwar photography contributed to the prestige of the Western movie of the 50s. Far from being a "low" form, it is one of the shared interests of both popular and elite tastes,[93] or was until television took it over. There has been change in Westerns, but McLuhan does not present the reasons.

The Western movie collapsed in the 60s largely due to the effect of television. Television Westerns ransack, conflate, and exhaust situations at high speed. The demands of the series format and the comparatively short running time of each program have returned new Westerns to a schematic narrative more like that of archaic silent movies than the expansive and complex development reached between 1947 and 1959 (the year of *Rio Bravo*). As argued above, the conventions were used as containers for elaborate shows of divided allegiance, psychological complexity, and ambiguous situations. The films that achieved this are now shown on television side by side with their parodistic progeny, and expressiveness is thereby lowered since at this stage the meaning of television as a whole is more interesting than individual items. (This seems to have been true of movies in the 30s when audiences apparently attended movie theaters regularly, whatever was showing.) New feature Westerns are few in number, and these are iconographically forced; three examples will indicate the problem. *El Dorado* has its heroes—John Wayne with a back injury, Robert Mitchum with a gunshot wound in the leg—squabbling about their crutches on the way to the final gunfight; *Five Card Stud,* 1968, tries to mix whodunit form with the out-in-the-open violence of the Western; and *Shalako,* with Brigitte Bardot, sets European aristocrats on a hunting trip among the Indians of the Southwest. Such ingenuities are labored compared with the clear flow of invention in earlier films made by the same men: compare *El Dorado* with Howard Hawks's *Rio Bravo, Five Card Stud* with Hal Wallis's crime films or his Jerry Lewis comedies, and *Shalako* with Edward Dmytryk's *Warlock.*

Under Roy Rogers' signature an article "What the Westerns Mean to Me" appeared in 1949. He wrote of his early work: "The plots hadn't changed much from the day Tom Mix was stalking the Sioux or Buck Jones was chasing the varmints to cover." The immaculate man and educated horse who visit crisis situations on a pilgrimage basis is now out of date, though it worked well as an accommodation of chivalric nostalgia with the formal requirements of a single-hero series. Television has revived the series form but has given the good-deed ethic of earlier series a more rational framework, such as an on-going wagon train that continually encounters new injustices or a marshal in one town to which the bad guys are irresistibly drawn.

Probably the main reasons for the sustained popularity of the genre are: first, that the Western is obviously derived from American history; second,

Hondo, Warner Bros. Pictures, Inc.

that it has the appearance of American style (in uniforms, in leisure wear, in posture); and third, it is a convention that assimilates current topics with astounding ease. As an example, let us consider a few significant treatments of William Bonney in the past thirty years; all the films are Westerns, but the emphasis of each is different. Robert Taylor played Billy the Kid in a 1940 movie of that name; Billy was of course a dark, taciturn, full-grown man just like the star. After the war, in *The Kid from Texas,* 1950, Audie Murphy played Billy; Murphy, then a chubby twenty-five-year-old, was a marine hero of World War II. Thus there was offscreen support for the youthfulness of appearance of the killer onscreen; real life—as it were—confirmed his youth in a way it did not confirm Taylor's maturity ten years earlier. Other films stressed the youth of Billy, notably *The Outlaw,* filmed 1940, first released 1943, in which he was played by Jack Beutel. The real age of Billy the Kid was given plausibility by young soldiers and even more by juvenile delinquents, who were a much publicized problem after World War II. The juvenilization of Billy culminated in *The Left Handed Gun,* 1958, in which the young Paul Newman played the part with a murderous playfulness influenced by Marlon Brando in *The Wild One* of five years earlier. Complementing this, movies from *The Gunfighter,* 1950 to *Forty Guns* and *The Lonely Man,* both 1957, stressed the difficulties of middle age in the profession of gunfighting. As a gunman says in *Forty Guns:* "The frontier is finished . . . I'm a freak." (Incidentally the problem of a lawman with failing sight is the gimmick of *The Lonely Man* and an incident in *Forty Guns.)*

The rhetoric of art discussion tends to require, as we have noted, personal authorship and a high level of permanence, criteria not easily satisfied in the popular cinema. There is, too, a related tendency to overrate originality at the expense of conventional elements in any art. This is particularly unhelpful in the discussion of movies, as our vocabulary is not designed to handle fixed and recurrent elements. It is the schematic parts, the symmetrical plots, the characters known beforehand and their geometrical relationships, that characterize the movies. These crystalline structures are set in a flowing naturalistic space and must be interpreted objectively if we are to get the point of a movie. A convention is always dominant; the extent to which the movies as a mass art accords with an accepted manner, model, or tradition, is the extent to which it will reach its audience. Our reflex homage to personal originality too often makes us dismiss as aesthetically negligible a formulaic film that may be an interesting, valid, even original development

within the convention. Internal, successive modification of forms rather than the display of individual control is a governing principle of popular culture.

Changes in the movies are cumulative. Consider what had been achieved with a highly conventional form by the movies of the late 40's. Without loss of the kind of clarity that Panofsky saw in the role of the butler in old mysteries, the iconography became dense, while retaining its essentially schematic contour. Take, again, *I Walk Alone,* in which Lancaster and Douglas compete for possession of a nightclub; or rather Lancaster wants his share and Douglas wants it all. Lancaster is old-fashioned, still thinking in terms of fourteen years earlier when he went to prison. Douglas has moved with the times and is protected not by muscle or weapons but by sophisticated accounting. The opposed characters change places when Lancaster uses the accountant's tool, a pen, hidden in his pocket to simulate a gun, which forces Douglas to resort to a real gun. These symmetrical diagrams of identity are not in the area of psychological exploration but in that of ironic situation. Situations and the location of known characters within suites and labyrinths of plot are functional in movies. In *Desert Fury* mother and daughter are sexually associated with the same man. It is an abrasive and memory-laden soap opera about gamblers and gangsters, with violence in the past and expected again at any minute. There is a final switch in which the gambler, representing power, is revealed as dependent on his companion whom he treats as a servant.

These are examples of the way in which Hollywood expanded schematic character into elaborate action in continuous spaces. Movies have avoided the psychologizing of the novel and drama of the 19th and 20th centuries. As Maurice Merleau-Ponty observes of images of man in the movies: "They do not give us his *thoughts,* as novels have done for so long, but his conduct or behavior. They directly present to us that special way of being in the world, of dealing with things and other people, which we can see in the sign language of gesture and gaze and which clearly defines each person we know . . . for the movies as for modern psychology, dizziness, pleasure, grief, love, and hate, are ways of behaving."[95] Movie iconography became increasingly complex but without the view of character becoming subjective. Freudian psychology was added to the characters' attributes, and an existential view of events destroyed the optimism of early movies. The poise and clear contour of primitive types was not lost, however. Critics attuned to the pursued and analyzed psyche naturally regard the movies' iconography of precise cues as shallow. On the other hand, to one adjusted to popular movies, the subjectivity of novels and plays may appear as a corrosion of action and plot (decision-making subverted by oscillating sensitivity). Alain Robbe-Grillet, discussing the adaptation of novels for films, observed: "Anyone can perceive the nature of the change that has occurred. In the initial novel, the objects and gestures forming the very fabric of the plot disappeared completely, leaving behind only their significations: the empty chair became only absence or expectation, the hand placed on a shoulder became a sign of friendliness, the bars on the window became only the impossibility of leaving. . . . But in the cinemas one sees the chair, the movement of the hand, the shape of the bars. As a matter of fact, it is as if the very conventions of the photographic medium (the two dimensions, the black-and-white image, the frame of the screen, the difference of scale between scenes) help free us from our own conventions. The slight 'unaccustomed' aspect of this reproduced world reveals, at the same time, the unaccustomed character of the world that surrounds us."[96]

Robbe-Grillet's point of the *solidification* of the world by the conventions of photography parallels Panofsky's concept of "photographed reality." The conventions of photography are exceptionally iconic, and because of our prior knowledge of this medium, we know this even when confronted by new configurations—provided they do not violate our normal perception of space, gravity, light sources. It is this relation of a solid image of the world with a flexible and receptive iconography that is unique to the movies. The world is not dematerialized even by dream sequences and flashbacks, because the past is another present with objects and figures. The difficulty of the popular film for critics lies precisely in the support that naturalism and iconography give to one another: the conventional becomes physically convincing and the known world a carrier of iconographical meaning. There is a fusion of "formulas of conduct" with "ephemeral configurations."[97]

There are precedents and analogues in the study of literary conventions. M. C. Bradbrook has discussed the plays in terms that are relevant to our argument. "The Revenge plays had a fixed narrative and fixed characters; consequently the speed of the intrigue steadily accelerated, yet the people would not feel the incidents to be incredible, though their effectiveness depended on their being extraordinary."[98] Bradbrook mentions the dramatists' reliance on "the Senecal tradition (which derived from the Italians) and the practice of greater dramatists like Kyd and Marlowe. In this way a body of incidents, types, tags grew up upon which anyone could draw."[99]

The Manchurian Candidate, United Artists.

Violence

"If you have not sufficient skill to make a sketch of a man throwing himself out of a window, in the time that it takes him to fall from the fourth floor to the ground, you will never be capable of producing great *machines.*" Delacroix, quoted by Charles Baudelaire, "The Life and Work of Eugène Delacroix," in *The Mirror of Art: Critical Studies by Charles Baudelaire* (Garden City, New York: Doubleday Anchor Books, 1956), translated by Jonathan Mayne. Originally published as a letter to the editor of the *Opinion Nationale* (Paris), 1863.

Traditionally there have been two sensitive subjects in the mass media, sex and violence, but now there is only violence. In movies, for example, sexual prohibitions have been relaxed for two reasons: primarily because of the social fact of greater permissiveness in conduct and dress and secondarily because of the competitive advantage for movies in showing more skin and in touching on yesterday's forbidden subjects, not yet available in family-bound television programs. The themes of violence in the mass arts have proliferated and intensified in the past twenty years, and the styles of the whole period are still viable, as is shown by the perpetuation of old films on television.

The political and social history of this period reveals great changes. It began with the first phase of the cold war, soon after the end of World War II, and includes the full show of doctrinal anti-Communism, in which John Foster Dulles represented its international and Joseph McCarthy its domestic form. The cold war permeated the mass media, as has been mentioned earlier; *Night People,* 1954, is typical of several movies that dealt with kidnapping and American counter-espionage activity along the Berlin Wall. The cold war did not survive the 60s, as a different view of communism developed and public violence took other forms. However, what the movies record is the continuance of violence as a social risk and human possibility through various shades of crisis. And certainly such topics as corrupt police (a series of scandals about big city police began in the late 50s) and crime as big business cannot be said to be outdated.

In the 60s emphasis moved from the image of Fortress America to that of Divided America. The movies, inasmuch as they combine topical references with long-term folkloric structure, are adaptable to both phases. If one defines violence in terms of territoriality, the spectacle on the screen conforms to either the external or the internal enemy. Violence can be defined as a series of distances and a schedule of gestures, moving toward a point at which we feel ourselves threatened or are threatening somebody else. The movies have defined both the topography and the timetable with exceptional precision. Movies have an almost complementary relationship to the news media, incidentally; where movies have a folkloric top level with an undercurrent of topical precision, news reporting tends to have a top level of topicality and a fund of covert folklore. In terms of the coverage of violent events, consider the handling of the shootings of Dr. Martin Luther King, Jr., in April and Senator Robert F. Kennedy in June 1968. The freewheeling anxiety and exuberance with which public deaths were discussed can be indicated by a quotation from *Newsweek:* "It almost seemed as if the shooting on Monday of Andy Warhol, the foremost creator of pop images, was a mad rehearsal, stage-managed by some diabolical cosmic impresario, for the shooting less than 48 hours later of Robert Kennedy, the most brilliant and mercurial political image of these days."[100] The two victims are linked by purely verbal devices—parallel adjectives such as "foremost" and "most brilliant"—and proximity, "Monday" and "48 hours later." I can see no connection between Valerie Solanis (who wounded Warhol) and Sirhan Sirhan. However, the assassination of President John F. Kennedy five years earlier is still endlessly discussed by conspiracy buffs who may speculate on the identity of the "cosmic impresario."

Another quotation will amplify the charged atmosphere of opinion about violence. *Time* magazine reported: "After Robert Kennedy's murder the Associated Press counted 199 Americans killed by gunfire in only seven days. The toll of citizen slaughter apparently rose even higher last week. In Manhattan's Central Park, across Fifth Avenue from Jacqueline Kennedy's apartment, a 42-year-old stock clerk named Angel Angelof waited inside a woman's lavatory,"[101] from where he shot passers-by at random before being shot down by the police. Note the emphasis that the introduction of the Kennedy name gives though in fact Mrs. Kennedy was away at the time; a solitary psychopath's act acquires hints of, if not conspiracy, at least a family curse. The public reaction to such overwritten reports, with the events glimpsed through a screen of sinister ornament, was naturally outrage and a desire for reform, but of what?

There are three possible explanations for all the killings: collective guilt, group conspiracy, and individual maladjustment: that is to say, sick society, secret societies, and individuals who may or may not have been influenced by the mass media.[102] If society is sick in a way that produces killings like these, a change in movie or television programming is unlikely to make much difference. Secret societies presumably operate without benefit of the mass media one way or the other. Although constantly under consideration, the threat of media causation has not been validated so far by research except in one special situation. It is important to distinguish between real and fictional violence. There seems to be no doubt that television coverage of riots *while they are occurring* can in fact precipitate more violence.[103] Instant coverage also legitimizes the actions of those taking part as they become news, transmitted to the biggest audience ever reached by one medium, and in so doing the news broadcasting may also attract fresh participants to the scene. The stimulus of violence in real time is not mediated by other values and other institutions, as is iconographically ordered violence.

In the absence of effective gun-control legislation, which is constantly delayed and sidetracked, the disturbed public looked for something within reach that it might influence. Following the assassinations, frustrated political and social hopes were diverted to an easy target, the mass media. Governor John R. Williams of Arizona appealed to the Western Writers of America to reduce gunplay in their books.[104] *Blackboard Jungle,* 1955, a knives-in-the-classroom movie with a rock-'n'-roll soundtrack, was canceled on television and replaced by a family film, *Sunday Dinner for a Soldier,* 1945.[105] Television companies reduced the number of Westerns and canceled (postponed?) the rougher episodes in series programs.[106] *McCall's* magazine took a full-page advertisement in *The New York Times* headed "What Women Can Do To End Violence in America" in which gun-control legislation and "the outpouring of violence and sordidness on our television screens and in the motion picture theaters" were equated; "mothers and grandmothers of this country" were urged to boycott "toys that foster and glorify killing."[107] This blatant piece of intermedia competition called, in effect, for vigilante action, exploiting liberal sentiment, bruised by current events. The demands that one makes of others, in the name of liberal feeling, were shown by one Hollywood mother's comment after Robert Kennedy's death. " 'My 6-year-old daughter was not shocked when she heard the news,' the actress Joanne Woodward recounted."[108]

The year 1968 was also that of the impact of *Bonnie and Clyde,* released in 1967. It was one of those films, which like *Rebel Without a Cause,* came to

symbolize a social problem: the sensibility of delinquency in one case and attitudes toward violence in the other. One film critic fought it from its first festival appearance to its New York premiere; another abhorred it and then retracted with a glowing palinode. *Time* and *Life* magazines used the same photograph of Faye Dunnaway as Bonnie being shot in the car at the end of the film to show how much violence we tolerate now. Ambiguous linkages of shocking fact and symptomatic fiction were numerous, as in this quotation from *Life:* "The shooting of Robert Kennedy increased the concern and the debate over the possible effects of the climate of violence that pervades today's world, where real life and fictional—as in the popular movie *Bonnie and Clyde*—are filled with images of brutality."[109] *Mad* satirized the film and a nudist magazine did a bare-skin takeoff in *The Jaybirders Present Bonnie and Clyde.*[110] The wide impact of the film was due in part to the revival of interest in 30s styles as well as to the guns and deaths.

Arthur Schlesinger, Jr., adapting without acknowledgment a phrase of Geoffry Gorer's, proposed the existence of "a pornography of violence."[111] He deplored in *Bonnie and Clyde* "its blithe acceptance of the world of violence—an acceptance which almost became a celebration."[112] Schlesinger's pamphlet was hastily written, and one sympathizes with the reaction of a public man to the assassination of two friends within a short time against a background of riot and undeclared war. Nevertheless, the special circumstances that led him to write the pamphlet may also have given his argument an undeserved authority.

What does the term "pornography" mean that would make it applicable to the mass media? If we take as pornography the photographs and literature collected by the Senate Subcommittee to Investigate Juvenile Delinquency in 1956,[113] we have a point of reference. The exhibits of the Subcommittee consisted of erotica of high specificity distributed clandestinely to a juvenile audience. On these terms we have a fair basis for deciding what is and what is not pornography. It is visual and verbal material that exceeds what is socially tolerable in significative form. The criterion needs to be a social one, because the standards vary from country to country and from one time to another in a single country. To the extent that erotic material is legally available, it is not pornographic: "pornography" is the name for unacceptable and illegal sexual depiction and description. During the 60s the code of what was permitted legally, especially in specialized magazines, changed fundamentally. The nude spoof of

Bonnie and Clyde, for instance, would have been inconceivable earlier; the visibility of the sexual organs would have been irreconcilable with parody. In less than a decade the level of what is permitted and what is not has fundamentally changed. Such variations are familiar in the history of censorship and ultimately make it impossible to arrive at an absolute definition of pornography. A social definition is the only one that can stand in the face of the variability of standards: "pornography" is that which must be clandestine for a particular group at a particular time.

Thus, to assert that a widely available and openly distributed film can be described by the same word as the Subcommittee's material is to stretch the term beyond the reach of reasonable discussion. Schlesinger argues that "we must recognize that the destructive impulse is in us and that it springs from some dark intolerable tension in our history and our institutions. We began, after, all, as a people who killed red men and enslaved black men."[114] It is true that America's history is savage, but what country's is not? If it is argued that American history has been bad recently (worse than that of Nazi Germany? or of the USSR?), what about the fact that Europe has a longer chronicle of violence and injustice? Schlesinger is on more secure ground when he observes, "one reason surely for the enormous tolerance of violence in contemporary America is the fact that our country has been more or less continuously at war for a generation."[115] Our involvement in World War II (1941–1945), Korea (1950–1953) and Vietnam (since 1965) could hardly fail to mark a society deeply. We know at first hand, ambiguously and bitterly, what it feels like to live in the century that Lenin predicted would be one of wars and revolutions.

In the place of a theory of national guilt we can propose a theory of self-awareness based on the American tendency to take the national pulse all the time. As the input of information increases, with data on war, economics, life expectancy, orgasms, delinquency, and everything else, what happens? In addition to the quantity of data, there is an increased subtlety in its interpretation. We are in a situation in which specialized information proliferates, and skepticism and anxiety tend to outpace the mastery of fact. American life is a drag strip of hotted-up crises. This aggrandized present induces anxiety partly because, by a curious twist, American practicality, the ethic that something can always be done, gives equal urgency to both marginal and central problems. The mass media's social effects have been subject to such a process of intensification. Daniel Bell, writing originally in the context of the liberal attack on horror comics in the 50s, pointed out: "In the last forty years or so, there has been the blurring, culturally and ecologically, of class lines. And in this blurring, in this spilling-over of classes, there has been not more violence but a greater awareness of the dimensions of living that include violence. With the rise of the movies and of other media, the growth of mass audiences, these 'windows' into the full range of life, from which the old middle class had been largely excluded, were extended."[116]

It is more than ten years since the public attack on horror comics, which resulted in their suppression; but in this time the level of public knowledge about the effects of mass communication has remained unaffected by objective research. Among the promoters of the idea of the media's ubiquity and evil, Frederick Wertham has the greatest celebrity. His attack on horror comics and its reflex acceptance represented a peak of liberal hysteria. Joseph Klapper observes that he "is probably the world's most voluble castigator of media-depicted violence, and in particular of comic books. Wertham claims to have diagnosed or treated numerous delinquent children in whose downfall comic books were the chief impetus. He does not seem to consider that emotional disturbance or abnormal aggressive tendencies are necessary prerequisites to comic-book influence but rather seems to believe, as the title of his best-known work asserts, that such fare in and of itself achieves *Seduction of the Innocents.* Wertham is not generally regarded, however, as having substantiated his very extreme views."[117] Is it not curious that a new generation of mass-media critics has not drawn on earlier research that would verify their assertions about the harmful effects of media violence? Question: did the removal of horror comics reduce delinquency and sibling mutilation in the 50s? If so the good news would surely have been reported and used against television.

"I remember the time when Disney and his less successful imitators concerned themselves with the frolicsome habits of bees, birds, and the minor furry animals," John Houseman wrote in 1947. "Today the animated cartoon has become a bloody battlefield through which savage and remorseless creatures, with single-track minds, pursue one another, then rend, gouge, twist, tear, and mutilate each other with sadistic ferocity."[118] It is true that cartoons reached a peak of violence in the late 40s, but the characters were almost always perennial, like Tom (the cat) and Jerry (the mouse);

each act of destruction was followed not merely by survival but by instant resurrection of the body. Houseman's view is no more extravagant than other fearful reactions to mass communications, but perhaps .the perspective of twenty years exposes the triviality of at least some panic reactions to violence. Before cartoons, radio serials were under suspicion, and afterward the problem was switched to horror comics; and now both movies and television are being reviewed. Common to each episode of public taste is a crudely simplified view of communication. The idea is that a scene, any scene, of violence transmits to the spectator a simple desire to act out literally what has been seen, heard, or read. This is too optimistic a view of the efficiency of human communications, which are subject to noise in the channel and to variable responses in different spectators.

The trouble with taking literally what you see on the screen, or read, can be exemplified by Sidney Hook's essay *The Fail-Safe Fallacy*. Filmed in 1964, *Fail-Safe* deals with an accidental nuclear attack on the USSR by the United States Air Force. Hook sees in the book's popularity "evidence of a widespread syndrome of political defeatism. It sees in the deterrent shield of defense, behind which the main centers of free culture have until now survived, an instrument not of safety but one that insures a world-wide calamity."[119] As popular culture has become more realistic, Hook argues, there is "a correspondingly great intellectual and moral responsibility to avoid fomenting hysteria."[120] In fact this book, like *Seven Days in May* or *The Satan Bug,* both of which were also filmed, cannot seriously be considered as socially harmful. They all represent popular art's calamity-oriented type; there is a fantastic play with institutions and a millennial game with coups d'etat, germ warfare, and nuclear exchange, but this is another form of fantastic topicality rather than of corrosive propaganda. Popular culture has considerable tolerance of irrational detail; the fixed symbols of the genre easily override causal explanation.

Public complaints about violence recur periodically, triggered by changing fashions in the media. The pattern of recurrence suggests that the present expression of concern is not caused solely by the political death and destruction of the late 60s, though these were certainly reinforcing factors. One source of the anxiety, I think, is what one might call the parent-teacher-librarian-columnist complex, and it is logical that it should arise among people in the roles of educators. The elite distrust of mass taste has been appropriated by the mem-

bers of the middle class most harassed through the media's "windows" by the spectacle of revealed violence. The "low" elements in entertainment, the insolent and passionate turns of pop culture, are offensive to that part of society accustomed to setting standards, but which no longer has the sole authority to do so. To attack the violence of movies and television is a protection of childish innocence and at the same time an assertion of authority over mass culture. Mass and child are equated; authority is claimed in a fusion of civic and parental roles. The position is one that earns easy agreement and has the advantage of locating the causes of violence outside the family. *Bonnie and Clyde,* and *Secrets of the Crypt* before that, are surrogates for the real problem.

The vulnerability of the hero has been mentioned as characteristic of postwar violent movies, either in the sense of a psychic flaw or as subjection to the same pains and injuries as everybody else, including the villain. We must also reckon with the decline in the prestige of being meek. In early films and dime novels, the biblical consolation that the meek should inherit the earth was a fundamental assumption. In later films the overbearing and the strong are, of course, defeated as often as they ever were, but by heroes who have become more like them. The experiences of 20th-century urban life have not confirmed the theory of compensatory rewards for passivity. Thus the perpetual violence in which the heroes are engaged is fundamentally adaptive rather than simply a personal aberration or a social disorder. It is true that violence is often presented as a flaw, but it is one that we all share, and if violence is renounced it is not until the end, as in *Point Blank,* 1967. Violence, of course, has long since exceeded the rules laid down in the past to regulate fights, and the hero is not usually a man who wins through brute strength. Violence is presented time and again as initiation, as the acquisition of skills. The techniques of violence are stressed, therefore, for the ambiguous equality that they confer: karate in *Johnny Cool* or marksmanship in *Seven Men from Now.* The pragmatic use of anything as a weapon is a point of *The Last Wagon,* in which Widmark uses rifle (from ambush), ax, knife, and revolver at various points of his revenge.

In the foreword to a bibliography on media problems edited by Wilbur Schramm the point is made that film and television experiences overlap. "It is safe to say that almost every important question raised by television research—addiction, effect on leisure-time, contribution to knowledge, effect of

Pickup on South Street, Twentieth Century-Fox Film Corp.

violence, relation to crime and delinquency, effect on mental adjustment, and so forth—was previously raised and considered in connection with the movies."[121] Hence research on the effects of one medium can often be legitimately transferred to the study of the other. It is relevant to quote here the conclusion of a study on *Television and the Child:* "the child's emotional make-up and the total of his environmental influences determine his behavior."[122] "The child's preferences in mass media reflect not only his age, sex, intelligence, but also his general outlook, spare-time interests, anxieties, and needs."[123] Serious research of the kind represented by this study, which reduces the effect of the media to one among a complex of factors, is popular neither with reformers nor with the entertainment industry. For their different purposes both groups act to inflate the power of the media, the reformers to keep their target big and simple, the entertainers to magnify the importance of their product.

What is needed in media research is first a contextual view of the experiences of representative members of the audience, and second a critical approach that does not break the continuities with earlier research. At present each new medium is ascribed the same problems that beset earlier channels. We are now, it seems to me, in a position to undertake the first task, thanks to the recent work of experimental psychologists. We already have the knowledge needed for the second task in the copious media and communication studies of American sociologists, but they have not reached a wide enough public. (The popularity of Marshall McLuhan's games of communication only delay the acceptance of historical and objective knowledge, for which they are a frivolous substitute.)

To consider the effect of violence in a movie on a given spectator, let us construct a three-phase situation consisting of: (1) predisposing factors; (2) contact in the theater; and (3) the post-viewing situation. In the first phase the spectator makes a choice of film, influenced by such factors as publicity, location of theater, and leisure time. The publicity, for any particular film including film reviews and other media references, serves as a kind of conditioning of the spectator, somewhat preparing him for what is to come. The period of contact is fairly complex; the spectator enters an environment constructed for the purpose of viewing films: off the street, into the lobby which acts as a transitional area, to the auditorium, dark and, sometimes, comfortable. Here, aside from audience interruptions (far fewer in number than at a play), the spectator

occupies an architecture of considerable privacy, insulated from the street. This privacy is not complete; there is an audience feedback which does not affect the actors, of course, but it does affect individual members of the audience. To see a film in, say, the suburbs and in a first-run theater are two very different experiences. To the preconditioning of publicity and to the conditioning of the viewing environment other sources of knowledge can be added: the spectator's pleasure will be influenced by preferences derived from his knowledge of other films, knowledge of other media, and learned social behavior. When he leaves the cinema the spectator returns to messages from other media of communication and to a world of non-media signals, social, familial, and personal. Lotte Bailyn has stressed the presence of "many mediating factors between exposure to material in the mass media and the translation of its influence into overt action."[124]

If a movie-goer is to be inspired to his own acts of violence by violent films, it can only be a movie-goer for whom the third phase, the post-viewing situation, is abnormal. That there are such individuals is certain, but it is not obvious that a change in movie content would normalize individuals who are already out of balance. I have argued for a correspondence between violence in the movies and the concurrent experience of society outside the theater, but such connections are not one-to-one. At the movies it is the recognition of topical material within traditional forms, the capacity of the norm to absorb new elements, that is a particular pleasure. The real defense against *Bonnie and Clyde* is the diversification of messages and attitudes outside the theater, the landscape of communications to which even the most infatuated spectator must return. Since society tolerates the extra activity in hospital emergency wards on Friday nights, payday, it is curious that the unverified stimulus to violence attributed to the mass media should cause such alarm.

The reason for the reformers' zeal has to do with the movies' connection with art. Violent and frightening subjects are traditional in art, but they have a traditional defender, Aristotle. In his *Poetics* the function of tragedy is defined as "by means of pity and fear bringing about the purgation of such emotions."[125] In its original form catharsis seems to have referred to the purging of the unmanly emotions of pity and fear themselves. Only later does it seem to have been modified to mean the exercise of these feelings in forms that enable us to respond morally to high occasions. In the "new and senti-

Top, *The Case Against Brooklyn,* Columbia Pictures Corp.
Bottom, *Pickup on South Street,* Twentieth Century-Fox
Film Corp.

Pickup on South Street, Twentieth Century-Fox Film Corp.

mentalized version of catharsis,"[126] low and trivial emotions are presumed purged by the stimulus of our capacity to pity and fear.

It seems clear that the movies do not do this, but what does? Leonard Berkowitz conducted a series of experiments to test aggression in subjects who had been exposed to violent stimuli. He summed up by observing that "the observation of aggression is more likely to induce hostile behavior than to drain off aggressive inclinations"[127] and more specifically, "The filmed violence was not cathartic."[128] Other experiments have led to comparable views: "Contrary to the catharsis hypothesis exposure of children to a film-mediated aggressive model increases the probability of their subsequently displaying aggressive behavior when aggression eliciting stimuli are present."[129] At the present time doubts about catharsis are reaching a climax; not only is its efficacy doubted by experimental psychologists, but the meaning of the term is unclear to skeptical literary critics. Works of art of antiquity and of the Renaissance, however brutal their subject, are protected by their prestige as cultural products. The theory of catharsis has provided the assurance of social usefulness to both pagan and Christian cruelties, to the flayings of both Marsyas and St. Bartholomew. The themes and images of violence in the mass media, lacking such cultural protection, have become the focus of the new suspicion that violence was not after all fully accounted for by Aristotle.

Aristotle wrote that "the best tragedies are written about a handful of families, those of Alcemaeon, for example, and Oedipus and Orestes and Meleager and Thyestes and Telephus."[130] In one respect the view has dated inasmuch as tragedies have been drawn from "low" families since the 18th century, but in another sense the observation is still true. These families were known to the Greek audience in a way comparable to the knowledge a modern audience has about the set iconographical conventions of movies. On a technical matter of this kind Aristotle's point is still legitimate, but in the evasive realm of audience psychology, in the study of affects, his ideas are untenable.

We are now historically in the position of facing the possibility that violence in all the arts is a non-cathartic spectacle. In fact, since the 16th century the idea of catharsis has been strained to accommodate ever rougher and more specific incidents. Cinthio's modification of the idea is mentioned above, and there is also Edmund Burke's straight statement that we enjoy witnessing suffering. His purpose was to define an aesthetics of awesome scenery, but his argument included tragedy and melodrama. "There is no spectacle we so eagerly pursue as that of some uncommon and grievous calamity . . . This is not an unmixed delight, but blended with no small uneasiness."[131]

The paradox of taking pleasure in pain is a recurrent and unsettled topic of literary and dramatic criticism. The movies, so often most fully visualized and articulate when the subject is violent, are central. The standard of *what may be enacted* has altered drastically since, for instance, Horace stipulated that "Medea must not butcher her children in the presence of the audience."[132] Yet we see and think we see such actions in the illusionistic cinema. Our experience of violent films, viewed in relation to the findings of experimental psychologists, casts doubt on the idea of purging by entertainment. It is the movies' sustained energy as an indigenous popular art that has revealed the weakness of our usual explanations for liking the spectacle of violence. The movies, as they have exceeded classical and genteel restraints, have gradually forced recognition of the inadequacy of catharsis theory by their status as a post-Aristotelian form, an insight that has implications for all the arts.

The Manchurian Candidate, United Artists.

Notes

There are various definitions in the text for which no source is given. All are from the unabridged *Random House Dictionary of the English Language* (New York: 1966).

1. Parker Tyler, *The Hollywood Hallucination* (New York: Creative Age Press, Inc., 1944).
2. Constance Rourke, *The Roots of American Culture and Other* Essays, edited, with a preface, by Van Wyck Brooks (New York: Harcourt, Brace and Company, 1942), page 290.
3. Reuel Denney, *The Astonished Muse* (Chicago: The University of Chicago Press, 1957), page 61.
4. Ian Fleming, *Thunderball* (New York: Signet, New American Library, 1962), page 75.
5. Daniel J. Leab, "Cold War Comics," *Columbia Journalism Review* (New York), III, 1965, pages 42–47.
6. *Ibid.,* page 42.
7. Bernard Bowron, Leo Marx, and Arnold Rose, "Literature and Covert Culture," in *Studies in American Culture: Dominant Ideas and Images,* edited by Joseph J. Kwiat and Mary C. Turpie (Minneapolis: University of Minnesota Press, 1960), page 84.
8. Damon Knight, "New Stars," *In Search of Wonder: Essays on Modern Science Fiction* (Chicago: Advent, 1967), page 203. Portions of this essay originally appeared in *Dynamic Science Fiction* (Columbia Publications, Inc., 1953).
9. James Agee, "Midwinter Clearance," *The Nation* (New York), February 14, 1948, page 192. Perhaps I should add that Manny Farber thought this one of Agee's good jokes.
10. Andrew Sarris, *The American Cinema: Directors and Directions,* 1929–1968 (New York: E. P. Dutton & Co., Inc., 1968), page 178.
11. André Bazin, "The Evolution of the Language of Cinema," *What Is Cinema?* Essays selected and translated by Hugh Gray (Berkeley and Los Angeles: University of California Press, 1967), page 30. A composite of three articles published 1950, 1952, and 1955.
12. Manny Farber, "Underground Films," *Commentary* (New York), November 1957, pages 432–439. © The American Jewish Committee. Reprinted in Daniel Talbot, ed., *Film: An Anthology* (Berkeley and Los Angeles: University of California, 1959), pages 163–74. Much of Farber's film criticism has been collected in *For Now #9* (Brooklyn), 1969, a special issue devoted to him.
13. Ernst Robert Curtius, *European Literature and the Latin Middle Ages,* translated by Willard R. Trask (New York: Pantheon Books, published for the Bollingen Foundation, Inc., 1953), page 81. Originally published as *Europäische Literatur und lateinisches Mittelalter* (Bern: A. Francke A G Verlag, 1948).
14. Raymond Durgnat, *Films and Feelings* (London: Faber and Faber Limited, 1967), page 268.
15. *Ibid.*
16. Tyler, *op. cit.* page 35.
17. Barbara Stanwyck, "Love Is a Gamble," *Screen Stars* (New York), vol. VIII, no. 2 1950, page 23. *(Thelma Jordan,* also known as *The File on Thelma Jordan,* was released 1950.) I am grateful to Ted Sutton for the opportunity to consult this and other popular magazines.
18. *Ibid.,* page 94.
19. "Antiquing We Will Go," *Screen Stars* (New York), vol. VIII, no. 2, 1950, pages 36–37.
20. "Love Gone Sour," *Hollywood Yearbook* (New York), vol. 1, no. 2, 1951, page 49. *Champion* was released 1949.
21. *Photoplay* (New York), vol. 40, no. 1, page 46.
22. Gustave Le Bon, *The Crowd: A Study of the Popular Mind* (New York: Ballantine Books, Inc., 1969), pages 45–46. Originally published as *La Psychologie des Foules* (Paris: 1895).
23. Cited in Herbert J. Gans, "The Creator-Audience Relationship in the Mass Media: An Analysis of Movie-Making," in *Mass Culture: The Popular Arts in America,* edited by Bernard Rosenberg and David M. White (Glencoe, Illinois: Free Press, 1957), note 14. It should be noted that Gans described the centripetal forces that pulled apart the film *The Red Badge of Courage.* In conflict were irreconcilable audience-images held by writer-director John Huston, studio production head Dore Schary, and producer Gottfried Reinhardt, caught in the middle.
24. Charles Higham and Joel Greenberg, *Hollywood in the Forties* (New York: A. S. Barnes & Co., 1968), page 15.
25. W. Stewart Pinkerton, Jr., "Fading Film Capital," *Wall Street Journal* (New York), June 27, 1969.
26. Higham and Greenberg, *op. cit.,* page 18.

27. *Vera Cruz* was filmed in Superscope, a wide-screen technique comparable to CinemaScope.

28. Pinkerton, *op. cit.*

29. Quoted by Roger Manvell, *New Cinema in the USA: The Feature Film since 1946* (London: Studio Vista Limited, and New York: E. P. Dutton & Co., Inc., 1968), page 26. No source is given.

30. Francois Truffaut, *Hitchcock,* with the collaboration of Helen G. Scott (New York: Simon and Schuster, 1967), page 14.

31. Bazin, *op. cit.,* page 34.

32. Higham and Greenberg, *op. cit.,* page 18.

33. Manny Farber, "Films," *The Nation* (New York), October 28, 1950, page 397. See note 12.

34. Stuart Byron, "Books," *The Village Voice* (New York), April 17, 1969.

35. Manny Farber, "Films," *The Nation* (New York), August 16, 1952, page 138. See note 12.

36. That the move was recognized for what it was and facilitated by Widmark's studio is clear from a picture story "Widmark the Movie Villain Goes Straight," *Life* (New York), March 28, 1949, pages 81–82, 85.

37. Farber, "Underground Films," *op. cit.,* page 432. *Stagecoach* was released 1939.

38. *Ibid.,* page 438.

39. *Ibid.,* page 436. Farber's article is, with James Agee's "Comedy's Greatest Era," probably the best piece of writing on American popular films, and Agee may have influenced its writing. Agee on Buster Keaton: "When he swept a semaphorlike arm to point, you could almost hear the electrical impulse in the signal block." Farber: "The control of Hawks's strategies is so ingenious that when a person kneels or walks down the hallway, the movement seems to click into a predetermined slot." Of Anthony Mann, Farber writes: ". . . the films of this tin-can De Sade have a Germanic rigor, caterpillar intimacy, and an original dictionary of ways in which to punish the human body." This sense of man as an object is a recurrent topic of film criticism (as of literary existentialism) and can presumably be linked with the nature of photographed reality. Agee's essay originally appeared in *Life* (New York), September 5, 1949, pages 70–82, 85–86, 88. Reprinted in *Agee on Film* (New York: McDowell, Obolensky Inc., 1958). It should be pointed out that Farber was not an uncritical admirer of Agee: see his "Stargazing for the Middlebrows," *The New Leader* (New York), December 8, 1959. See note 12.

40. André Breton, *Nadja,* translated by Richard Howard (New York: Grove Press, Inc., 1960), pages 32, 37. Originally published Paris: Librairie Gallimard, 1928.

41. Robert Desnos, "Imagerie moderne," *Documents* (Paris), vol. VII, 1929, page 377.

42. "André Malraux Talks to Roger Stéphane," *The Listener* (London), October 31, 1968, page 572. Translated by Nicholas Garnham.

43. Vincent Canby, "Which Version Did You See?" *The New York Times,* July 20, 1969.

44. Erwin Panofsky, "Style and Medium in the Motion Pictures," *Critique* (New York), vol. 1, no. 3, 1947, pages 27–28. Revision of article published as "Style and Medium in the Moving Pictures," 1934, Department of Art and Archaeology of Princeton University, subsequently published in *Transition* (New York), no. 26, 1937. Revised and brought up to date in *Critique.* All following references are to *Critique.*

45. Robert Warshow, "The Movie Camera and the American," *Commentary* (New York), March 1952, page 276. Reprinted in his collected essays, *The Immediate Experience* (New York: Doubleday & Company, Inc., 1962).

46. *Ibid.*

47. James Blue, "Excerpt from an Interview with Richard Grenier and Jean-Luc Godard," in *Jean-Luc Godard,* edited by Toby Mussman (New York: E. P. Dutton & Co., Inc., 1968), page 250. The original French title of *Contempt* was *Le Mépris.*

48. Truffaut, *op. cit.,* page 104.

49. *Ibid.,* page 199.

50. *Ibid.,* page 11.

51. Scenarios are by, respectively, Robert Alan Aurthur, Samuel Fuller, George Zuckerman, Orson Welles, Charles Schnee, and Jay Dratler.

52. Edward A. Shils, "Mass Society and Its Culture," in *Reader in Public Opinion and Communication,* edited by Bernard Berelson and Morris Janowitz (Glencoe, Illinois: Free Press, second edition, 1966), pages 508–528. He records that he also considered high, elaborate, genuine, or serious; middle; and low, base, or coarse.

53. See Paul Wember, *Die Jugend der Plakate: 1887–1917* (Krefeld: Scherpe Verlage, n.d.).

54. The term "expendable art," coined by Reyner Banham, was in use in London in the

second half of the 1950s. The fact that an art form is expendable does not mean that its history is not worth recording. On the contrary, at the College Art Association's annual meeting in 1968 one of the sessions was devoted to "Temporary Designs and Their Relation to the Permanent Arts."

55. Andrew Sarris, "The American Cinema," *Film Culture* (New York), Spring 1963, pages 46–47.

56. *Ibid.,* page 46. Peckinpah's stand is evasive. When asked "What did you think of the Budd Boetticher Westerns—*Ride Lonesome* and so on?" Peckinpah replied, "He did a great many with Randolph Scott. I saw one. I understand he's in Mexico now." "It's been alleged that *Ride the High Country* was a kind of summary of the Boetticher films." Peckinpah replied: "No, I think it came from N. B. Stone, who did the story and the screenplay." (Ernest Callenbach, interview with Peckinpah, *Film Quarterly,* winter 1963–64, page 3).

57. Curtis Lee Hanson, "An Interview with Burt Kennedy," *Cinema* (Beverly Hills, California), Spring 1968, pages 15–18.

58. Truffaut, *op. cit.,* page 142.

59. Dorothy Gardiner and Katherine Sorley Walker, eds., *Raymond Chandler Speaking* (London: Hamish Hamilton, 1962), pages 132–133.

60. *Ibid.,* page 135.

61. *Ibid.,* page 137.

62. *Ibid.,* page 135.

63. Curtis Lee Hanson, "An Interview with Don Siegel," *Cinema* (Beverly Hills, California), Spring 1968, pages 4–8; Tom Milne, ed., *Losey on Losey* (New York: Doubleday & Company, Inc., 1968).

64. Panofsky made the same comparison but with a different purpose. He used the cathedral as a model of group collaboration with "the role of the producer corresponding, more or less, to that of the bishop or archbishop," etc., whereas I propose it in relation to a relaxed requirement of formal unity. Panofsky, *op. cit.,* page 18.

65. Hanson, "An Interview with Burt Kennedy," *op. cit.,* page 17.

66. Mario Praz, "Shakespeare's Italy," *The Flaming Heart* (New York: Anchor Books, 1958), page 146. Essay first appeared in *Shakespeare Survey,* VII, edited by Theodore Spencer (Cambridge: Harvard University Press, 1931).

67. *Ibid.,* page 147.

68. E. F. Watling, introduction to Seneca, *Four Tragedies and Octavia* (Harmondsworth: Penguin Books, 1966), page 34.

69. *Ibid.,* page 35.

70. Praz, *op. cit.,* page 146.

71. Quoted in "Nerve Gas Accident," *Wall Street Journal* (New York), July 18, 1969.

72. Erwin Panofsky, "Iconography and Iconology: An Introduction to the Study of Renaissance Art," *Meaning in the Visual Arts* (Garden City, New York: Doubleday & Company, Inc., 1955), page 26. First published as "Introductory," *Studies in Iconology: Humanistic Themes in the Art of the Renaissance* (New York: Oxford University Press, 1939).

73. Panofsky, "Style and Medium in the Motion Pictures," *op. cit.,* page 14.

74. Panofsky, "Iconography and Iconology . . ." *op. cit.,* page 41.

75. *Ibid.*

76. Robert Warshow, "Movie Chronicle: The Westerner," *Partisan Review* (New York), March-April 1964, page 195. Reprinted, n. 45.

77. *Ibid.,* page 191.

78. Gardiner and Walker, eds., *op. cit.,* page 243. *The Big Sleep* was filmed in 1946, after other Chandler novels had been filmed. *Farewell My Lovely* was filmed as *Murder, My Sweet* in 1945, and before that another novel, *The High Window,* was made into a second feature called *The Falcon Takes Over,* 1942.

79. Ron Goulart, ed., "Introduction," *The Hard-boiled Dicks* (New York: Pocket Books, 1967).

80. Gardiner and Walker, eds., *op. cit.,* page 221.

81. *Ibid.*

82. Peter Bogdanovich, "Tashlin!" *Movie* (London), February 1963, page 15.

83. Mario Praz, "La Belle dame sans merci," *The Romantic Agony* (New York: Oxford University Press, 1951), pages 189–286.

84. Walter Pater, "Leonardo da Vinci," *The Renaissance: Studies in Art and Poetry* (Portland, Maine: Thomas B. Mosher, 1924), pages 162–163. First published *Fortnightly Review,* November 1869.

85. Peter Bogdanovich, "Working within the System, Interview with Donald Siegel," *Movie* (London), Spring 1968, pages 11–12.

86. Curtius, *op. cit.,* page 9.

87. Warshow, *op. cit.,* page 195.

88. Joseph T. Klapper, *The Effects of Mass Communication* (Glencoe, Illinois: The Free

Press, 1965), pages 170–171. The reference is to Frederick Elkin, "The Psychological Appeal of the Hollywood Western," *Journal of Educational Sociology* (New York), October 1950, pages 72–86.

89. *Ibid.,* page 171.
90. Andrew Sarris, ed., *Interviews with Film Directors* (New York: Avon, 1969), page 233. Translation by editor of an interview by Jacques Becker, Jacques Rivette, and Francois Truffaut, *Cahiers du Cinéma* (Paris), February 1956.
91. Marshall McLuhan, *Understanding Media: The Extensions of Man* (New York: Signet, New American Library, 1965), page 320.
92. *Ibid.*
93. See Allen Eyles, *The Western: An Illustrated Guide* (London: A. Zwemmer Limited, and New York: A. S. Barnes & Co., 1967) for an index of Western movies.
94. Roy Rogers, "What the Westerns Mean to Me," *Who's Who in Hollywood* (New York), vol. 1, no. 4, 1949, pages 52–53.
95. Maurice Merleau-Ponty, *Sense and Non-Sense,* translated by Hubert L. Dreyfus and Patricia Allen Dreyfus (Evanston, Illinois: Northwestern University Press, 1964), page 58. From a lecture delivered Paris 1945.
96. Alain Robbe-Grillet, *For a New Novel: Essays on Fiction,* translated by Richard Howard (New York: Grove Press Inc., 1965), pages 20–21. Originally published as *Pour un nouveau roman* (Paris: Les Editions Minuit, 1963).
97. The term "formulas of conduct" is adopted from Curtius, *op. cit.,* pages 79–105; and "ephemeral configurations" is one of the four properties of photography proposed by Siegfried Kracauer, *Theory of Film: The Redemption of Physical Reality* (New York: Oxford University Press, 1960), pages 18–20, the others being random events, endlessness ("fragments rather than wholes"), and the indeterminate ("multiple meanings").
98. M. C. Bradbrook, *Themes & Conventions of Elizabethan Tragedy* (Cambridge University Press, 1966), page 40. First edition 1935.
99. *Ibid.,* pages 4–5.
100. "The Sweet Assassin," *Newsweek* (New York), June 17, 1968, page 86.
101. " 'Insane and Reckless Murder'," *Time* (New York), July 12, 1968, page 18.
102. Jerry Landauer, "Does the Press Inspire Assassins," *The Wall Street Journal* (New York), July 18, 1968.
103. Morris Janowitz, "Patterns of Collective Racial Violence," in *Violence in America: Historical and Comparative Perspectives. A Report to the National Commission on the Causes and Prevention of Violence, June 1969.* Edited by Hugh Davis Graham and Ted Robert Gurr (New York: New American Library, 1969), pages 393–422.
104. "Western Writers Shoot Down No-Gunplay Pitch," *Variety* (New York), July 24, 1968.
105. "Violence on TV Heading for Fadeout," *The New York Times,* June 20, 1968.
106. "TV Oaters in Mesa Trouble," *Variety* (New York), July 17, 1968.
107. *The New York Times,* June 20, 1968.
108. "Understanding Violence," *Newsweek* (New York), June 17, 1968, page 46.
109. Albert Rosenfeld, "The Psycho-biology of Violence," *Life* (New York), June 21, 1968, page 67.
110. *Mad* (New York), June 1968; *The Jaybirders Present Bonnie and Clyde* (North Hollywood), July–September 1968, special issue.
111. Arthur Schlesinger, Jr., *Violence: America in the Sixties* (New York: New American Library, Signet Broadside, 1968), page 53. Geoffry Gorer, "The Erotic Myth of America," *Partisan Review* (New York), July–August 1950.
112. *Ibid.*
113. United States Senate, Interim Report of the Committee on the Judiciary made by Its Subcommittee to Investigate Juvenile Delinquency, *Obscene and Pornographic Literature and Juvenile Delinquency* (Washington, D. C.: 84th Congress, 2nd session, 1956 report no. 2381).
114. Schlesinger, *op. cit.,* page 31.
115. *Ibid.,* page 49.
116. Daniel Bell, "The Myth of Crime Waves," *The End of Ideology: On the Exhaustion of Political Ideas in the Fifties* (Glencoe, Illinois: Free Press, 1965), pages 173–174.
117. Klapper, *op. cit.,* page 290. Frederick Wertham, *Seduction of the Innocents* (New York: Rinehart, 1954).
118. John Houseman, "What Makes American Movies Tough?" *Vogue* (New York), January 15, 1947.
119. Sidney Hook, *The Fail-Safe Fallacy* (New York: Stein & Day, 1963), page 8.
120. *Ibid.,* page 32.
121. Wilbur Schramm, ed., *The Effects of Television on Children and Adolescents: An Annotated Bibliography* (Paris: 1964).
122. Hilde T. Himmelweit, A. N. Oppenheim, and Pamela Vince, *Television and the Child*

(New York: Oxford University Press, 1958), page 215.

123. *Ibid.,* page 150.

124. Lotte Bailyn, "Mass Media and Children: A Study of Exposure Habits and Cognitive Effects," *Psychological Monographs* (Washington, D. C.), vol. 73, no. 1 (whole no. 471), 1959, page 1.

125. Aristotle, "The Poetics," in *Classical Literary Criticism,* translated by T. S. Dorsch (Baltimore: Penguin, Pelican, 1967), page 39. The discussion of catharsis is in sections 6, 13, and 14.

126. William K. Wimsatt, Jr. and Cleanth Brooks, *Literary Criticism: A Short History* (New York: Alfred A. Knopf, 1957), page 207.

127. Leonard Berkowitz, "The Effects of Observing Violence," *Scientific American* (New York), February 1964, page 35.

128. Leonard Berkowitz, "Impulse, Aggression and the Gun," *Psychology Today* (Del Mar, California), September 1968, page 20.

129. Richard H. Walters and Donna C. Willows, "Imitative Behavior of Disturbed and Nondisturbed Children Following Exposure to Aggressive and Nonaggressive Models," *Child Development* (Chicago), March 1968, pages 79–80.

130. Aristotle, *op. cit.,* page 48.

131. Edmund Burke, *A Philosophical Enquiry into the Origin of Our Ideas of the Sublime and the Beautiful* (London: 1757), book 1, section 8.

132. Horace, "On the Art of Poetry" [1.185], in *Classical Literary Criticism,* translated by T. S. Dorsch (Baltimore: Penguin, Pelican, 1967), page 85.

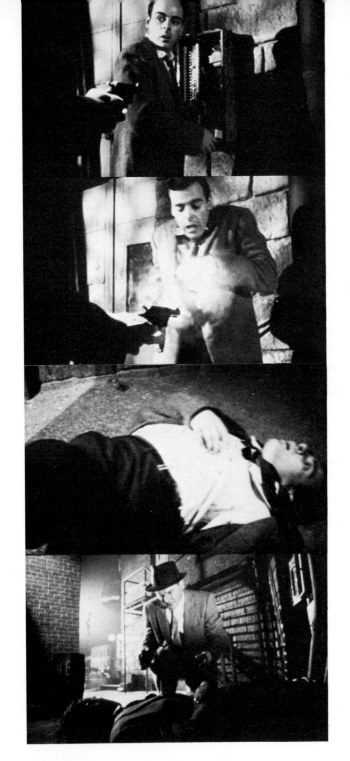

The Case Against Brooklyn, Columbia Pictures Corp.
Left column, a police wiretapper interrupted (1), shot by a
dishonest cop (2, 3), who searches the body (4); *right column,*
as the wiretapper's partner runs from the street (5, 6),
to fight the killer back along the alley (7, 8).

Appendix
The American Action Movie, 1946–1964

Credits of the films in the series originally shown at The Museum of Modern Art from April 24 to June 6, 1969, under the title *The American Action Movie, 1946–1964,* with excerpts from the program notes, follow. Portions of these notes have been incorporated in the text, so they have been omitted here. The order is chronological.

Title The Killers
Year 1946
Company Universal Pictures
Producer Mark Hellinger
Director Robert Siodmak
Screenplay Anthony Veiller
Source Short story by Ernest Hemingway
Photography Woody Bredell
special photography by D. S. Horsley
Editor Arthur Hilton
Music Miklos Rozsa
Running time 105 minutes
Cast

Burt Lancaster	Swede
Ava Gardner	Kitty Collins
Edmond O'Brien	Riordan
Albert Dekker	Colfax
Sam Levene	Lubinsky
Charles D. Brown	Packy
Donald McBride	Kenyon
Phil Brown	Nick
William Conrad	Max

The Killers is one of a number of violent movies directed by Robert Siodmak in the 40s, starting with *Phantom Lady,* 1944, and ending with *Criss Cross,* 1949, and *Thelma Jordan,* 1950. However, just as *Thelma Jordan* is strongly characterized by its producer, Hal Wallis, Mark Hellinger's hand is evident in the unremitting thoroughness of *The Killers.*

In addition, it is a writer's film. Ernest Hemingway's story is presented intact at the start of the film. It has the character of a set piece, with its laconic dialogue, stark situation, and bleak mood. The rest of the screenplay, written by Anthony Veiller, is an elaborate explanation of why the man killed at the start of the film had lost his will to live. In long flashbacks the past is explored to reveal, from several points of view, the events in the past that destroyed Swede's will to live. After *Citizen Kane,* elaborate flashbacks were standard in popular films. In *The Killers* the protagonist is an insurance investigator, tidying up after the murder. As played by Edmond O'Brien, he is flip and cocky in a 30s style, but the complex actions and concealed motives that he uncovers have a labyrinthine character typical of the dark films of the 40s.

Burt Lancaster was introduced in this movie, and Ava Gardner elegantly plays a fatal woman of extended duplicity. The film is organized so that at the end past and present converge, maximum violence and final explanation arrive together, blood and knowledge support one another. Contrary to what the escape theory of popular culture calls for, in this film, as in others of the period, mystery and action are used as framework for a melancholy and pessimistic view of life.

Title Desert Fury
Year 1947
Company Paramount Pictures Corp.
Producer Hal B. Wallis
Director Lewis Allen
Screenplay Robert Rossen
Source Serial by Ramona Stewart
Photography Charles Lang and Edward Cronjager
Editor Warren Low
Music Miklos Rozsa
Running time 95 minutes
Cast

John Hodiak	Eddie Bendix
Lizabeth Scott	Paula Haller
Burt Lancaster	Tom Hanson
Mary Astor	Fritzie Haller
Wendell Corey	Johnny Ryan
Kristine Miller	Claire Lindquist
William Harrigan	Judge Berle Lindquist
James Flavin	Sheriff Pat Johnson
Jane Novak	Mrs. Lindquist

Title I Walk Alone
Year 1947
Company Paramount Pictures Corp.
Producer Hal B. Wallis
Director Byron Haskin
Screenplay Charles Schnee
Source Play by Theodore Reeves, *The Beggars Are Coming to Town*
Photography Leo Tover
Editor Arthur Schmidt
Music Victor Young
Running time 98 minutes
Cast

Burt Lancaster	Frankie Madison
Lizabeth Scott	Kay Lawrence
Kirk Douglas	Noll Turner
Wendell Corey	Dave
Kristine Miller	Mrs. Richardson
George Rigaud	Maurice
Marc Lawrence	Nick Palestro
Mike Mazurki	Dan
Mickey Knox	Skinner
Roger Neury	Felix

Title	Out of the Past
Year	1947
Company	RKO-Radio Pictures
Producers	Warren Duff and Robert Sparks
Director	Jacques Tourneur
Screenplay	Geoffrey Homes
Source	Novel by Geoffrey Homes, *Build My Gallows High*
Photography	Nicholas Musuraca
Editor	Samuel E. Beetley
Music	Mischa Bakaleinikoff
Running time	97 minutes
Cast	
Robert Mitchum	Jeff
Jane Greer	Kathie
Kirk Douglas	Whit
Rhonda Fleming	Meta Carson
Richard Webb	Jim
Steve Brodie	Fisher
Virginia Huston	Ann
Paul Valentine	Joe
Dickie Moore	The Kid
Ken Niles	Eels

Title	Ramrod
Year	1947
Company	United Artists Corp.
Producer	Harry Sherman
Director	André de Toth
Screenplay	Jack Moffitt, Graham Baker, and Cecile Kramer
Source	Story by Luke Short
Photography	Russell Harlan
Editor	Sherman A. Rose
Music	Adolph Deutsch and Rudolph Pol
Running time	94 minutes
Cast	
Veronica Lake	Connie Dickason
Joel McCrea	Dave Nash
Ian MacDonald	Walt Shiply
Arleen Whelan	Rose
Don De Fore	Bill Schell
Preston Foster	Frank Ivey
Charles Ruggles	Ben Dickason
Donald Crisp	Sheriff Jim Crew
Lloyd Bridges	Red Cates
Rose Higgins	Annie
Chick York	Dr. Parks
Nestor Paiva	Curley
Cliff Parkinson	Tom Peebles
Ward Wood	Link Thomas
Trevor Bardette	Bailey
Wally Cassell	Virg Lee
John Powers	Pokey
Ray Teal	Burma
Hal Taliaferro	Jess Moore
Sarah Padden	Mrs. Parks
Jeff Corey	Bice

Title	The Lady from Shanghai
Year	1948
Company	Columbia Pictures Corp.
Producer	Orson Welles
Director	Orson Welles
Screenplay	Orson Welles
Source	Novel by Sherwood King, *If I Should Die Before I Wake*
Photography	Charles Lawton, Jr.
Editor	Viola Lawrence
Music	Heinz Roemheld and Morris Stoloff
Running time	87 minutes
Cast	
Rita Hayworth	Elsa Bannister
Orson Welles	Michael O'Hara
Everett Sloane	Arthur Bannister
Glenn Anders	George Grisby
Ted de Corsia	Sidney Broome
Erskine Sanford	Judge
Gus Schilling	Goldie
Carl Frank	District attorney
Louis Merrill	Jake

It is arguable that after Orson Welles's first films *(Citizen Kane,* 1941, *The Magnificent Ambersons,* 1942) his genre films are his best. *The Lady from Shanghai* and *Touch of Evil* (and even *Journey into Fear,* 1943 and *The Stranger,* 1946) have an authority and drive which prosper in the absence of Shakespeare or Kafka. *Mr. Arkadin,* 1962, an attempt to do *Citizen Kane* over again as a mystery story, falls apart and leads one to think that acceptance of the outline of a genre film may act as a ready-made container for Welles's extraordinary inventiveness. *The Lady from Shanghai* has the kind of plot, with double crosses and fall guys, causes separated from effects, and motives held in suspense, that made film critics of the period despair. Rita Hayworth, according to her motives and who's talking, is called Elsa, Rosalie, and Lover, which is typical of the film's multiplicity.

The end of the film, a shootout among the mirrors of a fun house, is celebrated, and a few of the last words of the movie are worth recording, not only as something Wellesian but for the exactness with which they catch the bitter mood of late 40s movies of violence. Elsa: ''Oh, Michael. I'm afraid. Michael, come back here. Please. I don't want to die.'' Michael walks out of the fun house, and the camera dollies high and back as his voice comes over his diminishing image: ''I'd be innocent officially, but that's a big word. Stupid is more like it.''

Title	D.O.A.
Year	1949
Company	United Artists Corp.
Producer	Harry M. Popkin
Director	Rudolph Maté
Screenplay	Russell Rouse and Clarence Greene
Source	Film directed by Robert Siodmak, *Der Mann, Der Seinen Morder Socht*
Photography	Ernest Laszlo
Editor	Arthur H. Nadel
Music	Dimitri Tiomkin
Running time	83 minutes

Cast

Edmond O'Brien	Frank Bigelow
Pamela Britton	Paula Gibson
Luther Adler	Majak
Beverly Campbell	Miss Foster
Lynn Baggett	Mrs. Philips
William Ching	Halliday
Henry Hart	Stanley Philips
Neville Brand	Chester
Laurette Luez	Marla Rakubian
Jesse Kirkpatrick	Sam
Cay Forrester	Sue
Virginia Lee	Jeanie
Michael Ross	Dave

Title	Sands of Iwo Jima
Year	1949
Company	Republic Pictures Corp.
Producer	Edmund Grainger
Director	Allan Dwan
Screenplay	Harry Brown and James Edward Grant
Source	Story by Harry Brown
Photography	Reggie Lanning
Editor	Richard L. Van Enger
Music	Victor Young
Running time	110 minutes

Cast

John Wayne	Sergeant John M. Stryker
John Agar	Pfc. Peter Conway
Adele Mara	Allison Bromley
Forrest Tucker	Pfc. Al Thomas
Wally Cassell	Pfc. Benny Regazzi
James Brown	Pfc. Charlie Bass
Richard Webb	Pfc. Shipley
Arthur Franz	Corporal Robert Dunne/Narrator
Julie Bishop	Mary
James Holden	Pfc. Soames
Peter Coe	Pfc. Hellenopolis
Richard Jaeckel	Pfc. Frank Flynn
Bill Murphy	Pfc. Eddie Flynn
George Tyne	Pfc. Harris
Hal Fieberling	Private "Ski" Choynski
John McGuire	Captain Joyce
Martin Milner	Private Mike McHugh
Leonard Gumley	Private Sid Stein
William Self	Private L. D. Fowler, Jr.
Dick Wessell	Grenade instructor
I. Stanford Jolley	Forrestal
David Clarke	Wounded Marine
Gil Herman	Lieutenant Baker
Dick Jones	Scared Marine
Don Haggerty	Colonel
Bruce Edwards	Marine
Dorothy Ford	Tall girl
John Whitney	Lieutenant Thompson
Colonel D. M. Shoup, U.S.M.C.	Himself
Lieutenant Colonel H. P. Crowe, U.S.M.C.	Himself
Captain Harold G. Schrier, U.S.M.C.	Himself
René A. Gagnon	Himself
Ira H. Hayes	Himself
John H. Bradley	Himself

Title	White Heat
Year	1949
Company	Warner Bros. Pictures, Inc.
Producer	Louis F. Edelman
Director	Raoul Walsh
Screenplay	Ivan Goff and Ben Roberts
Source	Story by Virginia Kellogg
Photography	Sid Hickox
Editor	Owen Marks
Music	Max Steiner
Running time	114 minutes

Cast

James Cagney	Cody Jarrett
Virginia Mayo	Verna Jarrett
Edmond O'Brien	Hank Fallon, alias Vic Pardo
Margaret Wycherly	Ma Jarrett
Steve Cochran	Big Ed Somers
John Archer	Philip Evans
Wally Cassell	Cotton Valetti
Mickey Knox	Het Kohler
Ian MacDonald	Bo Creel
Fred Clark	The Trader
G. Pat Collins	The Reader
Paul Guilfoyle	Roy Parker
Fred Coby	Happy Taylor
Ford Rainey	Zuckie Hommell
Robert Osterloh	Tommy Ryley

Title	In a Lonely Place
Year	1950
Company	Columbia Pictures Corp.
Producers	Robert Lord and Henry S. Kesler
Director	Nicholas Ray
Screenplay	Andrew Solt
Photography	Burnett Guffey
Editor	Viola Lawrence
Music	Morris Stoloff
Running time	92 minutes

Cast

Humphrey Bogart	Dixon Steele
Gloria Grahame	Laurel Gray
Frank Lovejoy	Brub Nicolai
Carl Benton Reid	Captain Lochner
Art Smith	Mel Lippmann
Jeff Donnell	Sylvia Nicolai
Martha Stewart	Mildred Atkinson
Robert Warwick	Charlie Waterman
Morris Ankrum	Lloyd Barnes
William Chang	Ted Barton
Steven Geray	Paul
Hadda Brooks	Singer
Alice Talton	Frances Randolph
Jack Reynolds	Henry Kesler
Ruth Warren	Effie
Ruth Gillette	Martha
Guy Beach	Swan
Lewis Howard	Junior

The theme of violence pervades *In a Lonely Place* with a minimum show of force. A series of detached wisecracks, bursts of temper, and a public brawl indicate a core of violence in a man by defining its outer edges. The idea mounts that it would not take much to slide from socially tolerable to outlawed violence. A murder investigation in which the central character is involved by chance provides an ominous parallel. All of this is smoothly managed by script and direction and by Humphrey Bogart's acting; it is one of his best performances, far superior to that in *The Treasure of Sierra Madre,* 1948.

This study of the estranging effects of violence uses a professional Hollywood background with sharp irony. In this respect the film belongs with *The Bad and the Beautiful,* 1953, and *Two Weeks in Another Town,* 1962 (both directed by Vincente Minelli and starring Kirk Douglas) for its disillusioned but infatuated self-image. These two Hollywood films deal respectively with a driving, manipulative character and with a bitter game between a director and an actor; both films teeter on the edge of violence like a drunk beside a swimming pool. In a comparable way *In a Lonely Place* deals with potential violence, with implications of savage action.

Title	The Steel Helmet
Year	1951
Company	Lippert Pictures
Producer	Samuel Fuller
Director	Samuel Fuller
Screenplay	Samuel Fuller
Photography	Ernest W. Miller
Editor	Philip Cahn
Music	Paul Dunlap
Running time	84 minutes

Cast

Gene Evans	Sergeant Zack
Robert Hutton	Private Conchie Bronte
Steve Brodie	Lieutenant Driscoll
James Edwards	Corporal Thompson
Richard Loo	Sergeant Budda-head Tanaka
Richard Monahan	Private Baldy
Sid Melton	Joe
William Chun	Short Round
Harold Fong	Korean major, The Red
Neyle Morrow	First GI
Lynn Stallmaster	Second lieutenant

Title	The Big Heat
Year	1953
Company	Columbia Pictures Corp.
Producer	Robert Arthur
Director	Fritz Lang
Screenplay	Sydney Boehm
Source	Serial by William P. McGivern
Photography	Charles Lang
Editor	Charles Nelson
Music	Mischa Bakaleinikoff
Running time	89 minutes

Cast

Glenn Ford	Dave Bannion
Gloria Grahame	Debby Marsh
Jocelyn Brando	Katie Bannion
Alexander Scourby	Mike Lagana
Lee Marvin	Vince Stone
Jeanette Nolan	Bertha Duncan
Peter Whitney	Tierney
Willis Bouchey	Lieutenant Wilkes
Robert Burton	Gus Burke
Adam Williams	Larry Gordon
Howard Wendell	Commissioner Higgins
Cris Alcaide	George Rose
Michael Granger	Hugo
Dorothy Green	Lucy Chapman
Carolyn Jones	Doris
Ric Roman	Baldy
Dan Seymour	Atkins
Edith Evanson	Selma Parker

Title	Hondo
Year	1953
Company	Warner Bros. Pictures, Inc.
Producer	Robert Fellows
Director	John Farrow
Second Unit Director	John Ford
Screenplay	James Edward Grant
Source	Story by Louis L'Amour
Photography	Robert Burks and Archie Stout
Editor	Ralph Dawson
Music	Emil Newman and Hugo Friedhofer
Running time	84 minutes

Cast

John Wayne	Hondo
Geraldine Page	Angie Lowe
Ward Bond	Buffalo
Michael Pate	Vittorio
James Arness	Lennie
Rodolfo Acosta	Silva
Lee Aaker	Johnny
Leo Gordon	Ed Lowe
Tom Irish	Lieutenant McKay
Paul Fix	Major Sherry
Rayford Barnes	Pete

Title	The Naked Spur
Year	1953
Company	Metro-Goldwyn-Mayer, Inc.
Producer	William H. Wright
Director	Anthony Mann
Screenplay	Sam Rolfe and Harold Jack Bloom
Photography	William Mellor
Editor	George White
Music	Bronislau Kaper
Running time	91 minutes

Cast

James Stewart	Howard Kemp
Janet Leigh	Lina Patch
Robert Ryan	Ben Vandergroat
Ralph Meeker	Roy Anderson
Millard Mitchell	Jesse Tate

Title	Pickup on South Street
Year	1953
Company	Twentieth Century-Fox Film Corp.
Producer	Jules Schermer
Director	Samuel Fuller
Screenplay	Samuel Fuller
Source	Story by Dwight Taylor
Photography	Joe MacDonald
Editor	Nick De Maggio
Music	Leigh Harline
Running time	80 minutes

Cast

Richard Widmark	Skip McCoy
Jean Peters	Candy
Thelma Ritter	Moe Williams
Murvyn Vye	Captain Dan Tiger
Richard Kiley	Joey
Willis Bouchey	Zara
Milburn Stone	Winoki
Henry Slate	MacGregor
Jerry O'Sullivan	Enyart
Henry Carter	Dietrich
George E. Stone	Clerk at police station
George Eldredge	Fenton
Stuart Randall	Police commissioner
Roger Moore	Mr. Victor
Frank Kumagi	Lum
Victor Perry	Lightning Louis
George Berkeley	Customer
Emmett Lynn	Sandwich man
Parley Baer	Stranger
Jay Loftlin	Librarian
Virginia Carroll	Girl in infirmary
Maurice Samuels	Peddler

Title	Suddenly
Year	1954
Company	United Artists Corp.
Producer	Robert Bassler
Director	Lewis Allen
Screenplay	Richard Sale
Photography	Charles Clarke
Editor	John Schreyer
Music	David Raskin
Running time	75 minutes

Cast

Frank Sinatra	John Baron
Sterling Hayden	Tod Shaw
James Gleason	Pop Benson
Christopher Dark	Bart Wheeler
Paul Frees	Benny Conklin
Nancy Gates	Ellen Benson
Kim Charney	Pidge Benson
Willis Bouchey	Dan Carney

Ken Dibbs	Wilson
Clark Howatt	Haggerty
James Lilburn	Jud Hobson
Charles Smith	Bebop
Paul Wexler	Slim Adams
Dan White	Burge
Richard Collier	Hawkins
Roy Engel	Driver number 1
Ted Stanhope	Driver number 2
Charles Waggenheim	Kaplan

"Suddenly" is the name of a small town in California at which a train carrying the President of the United States is scheduled to stop. A hired assassin, an American who is no more troubled by patriotism than Richard Widmark's pickpocket in *Pickup on South Street,* arrives with a rifle. In opposition to those movies that assume the corruption of cities, even small ones, as in *The Tattered Dress,* for example, *Suddenly* deals with the occupation of a house in a virtuous place by outside hoodlums. As in *The Night Holds Terror* and *The Desperate Hours,* both 1955, with John Cassavetes and Humphrey Bogart respectively as the invaders, life as routine (defined in opening credits of *Suddenly)* is interrupted by the threat of violent death.

The chief convention of *Suddenly,* extended from the explanatory endings of innumerable crime films, is that bad guys love to talk. Frank Sinatra paces about and talks on and on; under the shower of words the hostages wilt or scheme. Some of the sociology of resentment written for him by Richard Sale is somewhat dated, but the image of a bitter man wrapped in his monologue is well done by Sinatra and by the straightforward narrative. The camera is not confined to the house, but the excursions outside the house are not ambulatory trips for relief but rather act as businesslike extensions of narrative.

Title	House of Bamboo
Year	1955
Company	Twentieth Century-Fox Film Corp.
Producer	Buddy Adler
Director	Samuel Fuller
Screenplay	Harry Kleiner
Additional dialogue	Samuel Fuller
Photography	Joe MacDonald
Editor	James B. Clarke
Music	Leigh Harline
Running time	102 minutes
Cast	
Robert Ryan	Sandy Dawson
Robert Stack	Eddie Spanier
Shirley Yamaguchi	Mariko
Cameron Mitchell	Griff
Brad Dexter	Captain Hanson
Sessue Hayakawa	Inspector Kita

Biff Elliot	Webber
Sandro Giglio	Ceram
Elko Hanabusa	Screaming woman
Harry Carey, Jr.	John
Peter Gray	Willy
Robert Quarry	Phil
De Forest Kelley	Charlie
John Doucette	Skipper
Teru Shimada	Nagaya
Robert Hosoi	Doctor
May Takasugi	Bath attendant
Robert Okazaki	Mr. Hommaru
Jack Maeshiro	Bartender

Title	Kiss Me Deadly
Year	1955
Company	United Artists Corp.
Producer	Robert Aldrich
Director	Robert Aldrich
Screenplay	A. I. Bezzerides
Source	Novel by Mickey Spillane
Photography	Ernest Laszlo
Editor	Mike Luciano
Music	Frank DeVol
Running time	105 minutes
Cast	
Ralph Meeker	Mike Hammer
Albert Dekker	Dr. Soberin
Paul Stewart	Carl Eyello
Juano Hernandez	Eddie Yaeger
Wesley Addy	Pat
Marian Carr	Friday
Maxine Cooper	Velda
Cloris Leachman	Christina
Gaby Rodgers	Lily Carver
Nick Dennis	Nick
Jack Lambert	Sugar
Jack Elam	Charlie Max
Jerry Zinneman	Sammy
Leigh Snowden	Girl at pool
Percy Helton	Morgue doctor
Madi Comfort	Night club singer
Fortunio Bonavona	Trivaco
James McCallian	Super
Silvio Minciotti	Old man
Robert Cornthwaite	FBI man
James Seay	FBI man
Mara McAfee	Nurse
Mort Marshall	Diker
Jesslyn Fax	Mrs. Super

The film is jammed with character actors, Greeks and Italians, cops and gunmen, doctors and janitors, chicks and desk clerks. They are stereotyped, but the stereotypes are so numerous and emphatic that they add up to a real crowd.

They are presented on the small black-and-white screen with a dense but easy patterning. It is a kind of deliberate revival of a brisk and eventful style of the 40s which by 1955 was somewhat under pressure from the long takes and tranquil spaces of the big screens. (Samuel Fuller's *Underworld USA*, 1961, has a comparable historicist detailing as does his more economically created tension in *Pickup on South Street.*)

Title The Phenix City Story
Year 1955
Company Allied Artists Pictures Corporation
Producer Sam Bischoff and David Diamond
Director Phil Karlson
Screenplay Crane Wilbur and Dan Mainwaring
Photography Harry Neumann
Editor George White
Music Harry Sukman
Running time 100 minutes
Cast

John McIntire	Albert Patterson
Richard Kiley	John Patterson
Kathryn Grant	Ellie Rhodes
Edward Andrews	Rhett Tanner
James Edwards	Zeke Ward
Lenka Peterson	Mary Jo Patterson
Biff McGuire	Fred Gage
Truman Smith	Ed Gage
Jean Carson	Cassie
Meg Myles	Judy
Katharine Marlowe	Mamie
John Larch	Clem Wilson
Allen Nourse	Jeb Bassett
Helen Martin	Helen Ward
Otto Hulett	Hugh Bentley
George Mitchell	Hugh Britton
Ma Beachie	Herself
James Ed Seymour	Himself
Clete Roberts	Reporter in prologue

Title Attack!
Year 1956
Company United Artists Corp.
Producer Robert Aldrich
Director Robert Aldrich
Screenplay James Poe
Source Play by Norman Brooks, *The Fragile Fox*
Photography Joseph Biroc
Editor Michael Luciano
Music Frank DeVol
Running time 107 minutes
Cast

Jack Palance	Lieutenant Costa
Eddie Albert	Captain Cooney
Lee Marvin	Colonel Bartlett
Robert Strauss	Pfc. Bernstein
Richard Jaeckel	Pfc. Snowden
Buddy Ebsen	Sergeant Tolliver
William Smithers	Lieutenant Woodruff
Jon Shepodd	Corporal Jackson
James Goodwin	Pfc. Ricks
Peter Van Eyck	Tall German
Steven Geray	Short German
Judson Taylor	Pfc. Abramowitz
Louis Mercier	Old Frenchman
Strother Martin	Sergeant Ingersol

Title Backlash
Year 1956
Company Universal Pictures
Producer Aaron Rosenberg
Director John Sturges
Screenplay Borden Chase
Source Novel by Frank Gruber
Photography Irving Glassberg
Editor Sherman Todd
Music Herman Stein
Running time 83 minutes
Cast

Richard Widmark	Jim Slater
Donna Reed	Karyl Orton
John McIntire	Jim Bonniwell
William Campbell	Johnny Cool
Barton MacLane	Sergeant Lake
Harry Morgan	Tony Welker
Robert J. Wilke	Jeff Welker
Jack Lambert	Benton
Roy Roberts	Major Carson
Edward C. Platt	Sheriff Marson
Robert Foulk	Sheriff Olson
Phil Chambers	Dobbs
Gregg Barton	Sleepy
Fred Graham	Ned McCloud
Frank Chase	Cassidy

Note the name of the character played by William Campbell. His role is that of a narcissistic killer whom Widmark disposes of by shooting in the head in a gun duel. The name *Johnny Cool* was picked up in 1963 as a film title and refers to another narcissistic killer, becoming a nickname for Johnny Coleano.

Title	The Last Wagon
Year	1956
Company	Twentieth Century-Fox Film Corp.
Producer	William B. Hawks
Director	Delmer Daves
Screenplay	James Edward Grant, Delmer Daves, and Gwen Bagni Gielgud
Source	Screen story by Gwen Bagni Gielgud
Photography	Wilfrid Cline
Editor	Hugh S. Fowler
Music	Lionel Newman
Running time	98 minutes

Cast

Richard Widmark	Todd
Felicia Farr	Jenny
Susan Kohner	Jolie
Tommy Rettig	Billy
Stephanie Griffin	Valinda
Ray Stricklyn	Clint
Nick Adams	Ridge
Carl Benton Reid	General Howard
Douglas Kennedy	Colonel Normand
George Mathews	Bull Harper
James Drury	Lieutenant Kelly
Ken Clark	Sergeant
Timothy Carey	Cole Harper
George Ross	Sarge
Juney Ellis	Mrs. Clinton
Abel Fernandez	Apache medicine man

Title	Seven Men from Now
Year	1956
Company	Warner Bros. Pictures, Inc.
Producers	Andrew V. McLaglen and Robert E. Morrison for Batjac Productions
Director	Budd Boetticher
Screenplay	Burt Kennedy
Photography	William H. Clothier
Editor	Everett Sutherland
Music	Henry Vars
Running time	77 minutes

Cast

Randolph Scott	Stride
Gail Russell	Annie
Lee Marvin	Masters
Walter Reed	Greer
John Larch	Bodeen
Donald Barry	Clete
Fred Graham	Henchman
John Barradino	Clint
John Phillips	Jed
Chuck Roberson	Mason
Steve Mitchell	Fowler
Pamela Duncan	Señorita
Stuart Whitman	Cavalry lieutenant

Title	Written on the Wind
Year	1956
Company	Universal Pictures
Producer	Albert Zugsmith
Director	Douglas Sirk
Screenplay	George Zuckerman
Source	Novel by Robert Wilder
Photography	Russell Metty with Clifford Stine
Editor	Russell F. Schoengarth
Music	Frank Skinner
Running time	99 minutes

Cast

Rock Hudson	Mitch Wayne
Lauren Bacall	Lucy Moore Hadley
Robert Stack	Kyle Hadley
Dorothy Malone	Marylee Hadley
Robert Keith	Jasper Hadley
Grant Williams	Biff Miley
Robert J. Wilke	Dan Willis
Edward C. Platt	Dr. Paul Cochrane
Harry Shannon	Hoak Wayne
John Larch	Roy Carter
Roy Glenn	Sam
Maidie Norman	Bertha
Dani Crayne	Blonde girl
Jane Howard	Woman drinking beer
Floyd Simmons	Man drinking beer
Cynthia Patrick	Waitress
Colleen McClatchey	College girl
Joanne Jordan	Brunette girl
William Schallert	Reporter
Robert Brubaker	Hotel manager
Bert Holland	Court clerk
Don C. Harvey	Taxi starter
Carl Christian	Bartender
Joseph Granby	R. J. Courtney
Gail Bonney	Hotel floorlady
Paul Bradley	Maitre d'
Susan Odin	Marylee as a girl
Robert Lyden	Kyle as a boy
Robert Winans	Mitch as a boy
Dorothy Porter	Secretary
Robert Malcolm	Hotel proprietor

Written on the Wind is a soap opera at the edge of violence, a family drama zigzagging like a fast car along the yellow lines. It is the product of a concentration of skills, from Albert Zugsmith, the producer (compare his *Tattered Dress* with the same writer, George Zuckerman) to the director Douglas Sirk. In the 50s, Sirk made for Universal a series of elegant, tearful movies (from *All I Desire,* 1954, to *Imitation of Life,* 1959). For Zugsmith again he made *The Tarnished Angels,* 1958, a good version of William Faulkner's *Pylon.*

In this film the stresses and final tearing apart of a rich oil family are displayed with a marvelous blend of schematic situation and lavish detailing. Sirk is a master of the consumer's world, of shiny cars, of long tables set for dinner, of wardrobes stacked with clothes. He handles such material with sensuous relish, but the wardrobe is for seduction and in the pastel-colored bedroom the baby is aborted after the father's violence. Robert Stack's hysteria and Rock Hudson's aplomb are circled by the delirium of Dorothy Malone and the devotion of Lauren Bacall. A detail typical of the film's mixture of threat and opulence is Bacall's discovery of a gun under her husband's pillow on their honeymoon. The mixture of family drama and physical violence in *Written on the Wind* is a 50s version of similar elements in *Desert Fury.*

The Big Heat, The Case Against Brooklyn, and *The Tattered Dress,* of this period also deal with aspects of the theme.

The names of the antagonists indicate the schematic intensity of the film: Ben Sadler, a name redolent of virtue, is the sheriff who insists on investigating violent death, even a Mexican's. Virgil Renchler (Welles at his grossest and most absent-minded) is the big rancher who tolerates murder— if it's a Mexican's. In one way the film is the opposite of *Touch of Evil* with its fluent and involved action in deep space. Jack Arnold's characters stand about at focal points almost like chessmen, and simple patterns of light and shade cross the screen with a billboard's emphasis; such a use of the CinemaScope screen (see also his film *The Tattered Dress*) is fully appropriate to the insistent pattern of conflict in the situation. Jeff Chandler's sheriff, physically battered and socially isolated, is a hero of the period, morally committed and physically vulnerable.

Title	Man in the Shadow
Year	1957
Company	Universal Pictures
Producer	Albert Zugsmith
Director	Jack Arnold
Screenplay	Gene L. Coon
Source	Story by Gene L. Coon
Photography	Arthur E. Arling
Editor	Edward Curtiss
Music	Joseph Gershenson
Running time	80 minutes
Cast	
Jeff Chandler	Ben Sadler
Orson Welles	Virgil Renchler
Colleen Miller	Skippy Renchler
Ben Alexander	Ab Bengley
Barbara Lawrence	Helen Sadler
John Larch	Ed Yates
James Gleason	Hank James
Royal Dano	Aiken Clay
Paul Fix	Herb Parker
Leo Gordon	Chet Huneker
Martin Garralaga	Jesus Cisneros
Mario Siletti	Tony Santoro
Charles Horvath	Len Bookman
William Schallert	Jim Shaney
Joseph J. Greene	Harry Youngquist
Forrest Lewis	Jake Kelley
Harry Harvey, Sr.	Dr. Creighton
Joe Schneider	Juan Martin
Mort Mills	Gateman

Title	The Tall T
Year	1957
Company	Columbia Pictures Corp.
Producer	Randolph Scott and Harry Joe Brown
Director	Budd Boetticher
Screenplay	Burt Kennedy
Source	Story by Elmore Leonard
Photography	Charles Lawton, Jr.
Editor	Al Clark
Music	Heinz Roemheld
Running time	78 minutes
Cast	
Randolph Scott	Pat Brennan
Richard Boone	Usher
Maureen O'Sullivan	Doretta Mims
Arthur Hunnicutt	Ed Rintoon
Skip Homeier	Billy Jack
Henry Silva	Chink
John Hubbard	William Mims
Robert Burton	Tenvoorde
Robert Anderson	Jace
Fred E. Sherman	Hank Parker
Chris Olsen	Jeff

Man in the Shadow is supposedly part of an agreement made by Albert Zugsmith and Orson Welles: in return for directing *Touch of Evil*, Welles reportedly agreed to act in this film. Zugsmith produced both films, each one dealing with murder against a background of racial problems: here, the abuse of Mexican migrant workers; in *Touch of Evil* the clash of a Mexican and an Irish cop during a murder investigation in a border town. Gene L. Coon wrote the script on the basis of a mastery of the then-present level of corrupt city iconography.

Title	The Tattered Dress
Year	1957
Company	Universal Pictures
Producer	Albert Zugsmith
Director	Jack Arnold
Screenplay	George Zuckerman
Photography	Carl E. Guthrie with Clifford Stine
Editor	Edward Curtiss
Music	Frank Skinner
Running time	93 minutes
Cast	
Jeff Chandler	James Gordon Blane
Jeanne Crain	Diane Blane
Jack Carson	Nick Hoak
Gail Russell	Carol Morrow
Elaine Stewart	Charleen Reston
George Tobias	Billy Giles
Edward Andrews	Lester Rawlings
Philip Reed	Michael Reston
Edward C. Platt	Ralph Adams
Paul Birch	Frank Mitchell
Alexander Lockwood	Paul Vernon
Edwin Jerome	Judge
William Schallert	Court clerk
June McCall	Girl at slot machine
Frank Scannell	Cal Morrison
Floyd Simmons	Larry Bell
Ziva Shapir	Woman on train
Marina Orschel	Girl by pool
Ingrid Goude	Girl by pool

Title	The Case Against Brooklyn
Year	1958
Company	Columbia Pictures Corp.
Producer	Charles H. Schneer
Director	Paul Wendkos
Screenplay	Raymond T. Marcus
Adaptation	Daniel B. Ullman
Source	Article by Ed Reid, "I Broke the Brooklyn Graft Scandal"
Photography	Fred Jackman
Editor	Edwin Bryant
Music	Mischa Bakaleinikoff
Running time	82 minutes
Cast	
Darren McGavin	Pete Harris
Maggie Hayes	Lil Polombo
Warren Stevens	Rudi Franklin
Peggy McCay	Jane Harris
Tol Avery	Michael W. Norris
Emile Meyer	Captain P. T. Willis
Nestor Paiva	Finelli
Brian Hutton	Jess Johnson
Robert Osterloh	Bonney
Joseph Turkel	Monte

Thomas B. Henry	Edmondson
Cheerio Meredith	Mrs. Carney

A Western of 1959, *Face of a Fugitive,* directed by Paul Wendkos, is another film in which a genre form is used to investigate paradoxes of identity. As in *The Case Against Brooklyn* the final shootout has the hero wounded and almost passive on the floor. The theme of the battered and divided hero, which recurs in movies of the 50s, receives a highly intense characterization in these two films. Details: the space of a small room nicely defined by a heavyweight fight of hero and two men; a long shot of a figure running from distance to close-up after the shooting in an alley.

Title	The Left Handed Gun
Year	1958
Company	Warner Bros. Pictures Corp.
Producer	Fred Coe
Director	Arthur Penn
Screenplay	Leslie Stevens
Source	Television play by Gore Vidal, *The Death of Billy the Kid*
Photography	J. Peverell Marley
Editor	Folmar Blangsted
Music	Alexander Courage
Running time	105 minutes
Cast	
Paul Newman	Billy Bonney
Lita Milan	Celsa
John Dehner	Pat Garrett
Hurd Hatfield	Moultrie
James Congdon	Charlie Boudre
James Best	Tom Folliard
Colin Keith-Johnston	Turnstall
John Dierkes	McSween
Bob Anderson	Hill
Wally Brown	Moon
Ainslie Pryor	Joe Grant
Martin Garralaga	Saval
Denver Pyle	Ollinger
Paul Smith	Bell
Nestor Paiva	Maxwell
Jo Summers	Mrs. Garrett
Robert Foulk	Brady
Anne Barton	Mrs. Hill

Title	The Lineup
Year	1958
Company	Columbia Pictures Corp.
Producers	Jaime Del Valle
Director	Don Siegel
Screenplay	Stirling Silliphant
Source	Based on the television series *The Lineup* by Lawrence L. Klee
Photography	Hal Mohr
Editor	Al Clark
Music	Mischa Bakaleinikoff
Running time	86 minutes

Cast

Eli Wallach	Dancer
Robert Keith	Julian
Warner Anderson	Lieutenant Guthrie
Richard Jaeckel	Sandy McLain
Mary La Roche	Dorothy Bradshaw
William Leslie	Larry Warner
Emile Meyer	Inspector Quine
Marshall Reed	Inspector Asher
Raymond Bailey	Philip Dressler
Vaughn Taylor	The Man (Mr. Big)
Cheryl Calloway	Cindy
Bert Holland	Porter
George Eldredge	Dr. Turkel
Robert Bailey	Staples

San Francisco has been used many times in the topography of violence, for example, *The Lady from Shanghai, The Sniper,* 1951, and *Bullitt,* 1968. The sharpest and fastest of the violent films to use this location is *The Lineup.* The opening is typical of the best handling of action (see page 90). The whole thing feels as though it takes no time at all. It is a montage based on accelerated action, not on temporal delay nor symbolic reinforcement in the manner of Soviet films. It is the compression of continuous action as in the final gunfight in the bar in *The Killers,* 1946.

The camera, though it indicates the inquiries of custom and police, spends most of its time with a pair of killers who have arrived in San Francisco with a list of targets. Gradually the police and the killers converge for a final car chase ending on an unfinished highway. However, bad luck and a failure of professional conduct on the part of one of the killers have already been fatal for the killers who would have been destroyed by the Syndicate anyway. Instead of an overt moral judgment on the killers, who may have a homosexual relationship, failure is simply an acknowledgment of the hazards of a high-risk profession. Donald Siegel elaborated the killers as the foreground characters of a later film, the 1964 version of *The Killers.*

For purposes of promotion the film was said to be based on a television program of the 50s, but it is in fact an original screenplay.

Title	Touch of Evil
Year	1958
Company	Universal Pictures
Producer	Albert Zugsmith
Director	Orson Welles
Screenplay	Orson Welles
Source	Novel by Whit Masterson, *Badge of Evil*
Photography	Russell Metty
Editors	Virgil Vogel and Aaron Stell
Music	Henry Mancini
Running time	95 minutes

Cast

Charlton Heston	Ramon Miguel (Mike) Vargas
Janet Leigh	Susan Vargas
Orson Welles	Hank Quinlan
Joseph Calleia	Pete Menzies
Akim Tamiroff	Uncle Joe Grandi
Joanna Moore	Marcia Linnekar
Ray Collins	Adair
Dennis Weaver	The Night Man
Valentin De Vargas	Pancho
Mort Mills	Schwartz
Victor Millan	Manelo Sanchez
Lalo Rios	Risto
Michael Sargent	Pretty Boy
Guest Stars	Marlene Dietrich
	Zsa Zsa Gabor
Uncredited appearances	Joseph Cotten
	Mercedes McCambridge

Touch of Evil is perhaps the best of Welles' later films. One reason for its quality may be related to its genre status, that of violence with social problems. The ready-made structure gives a tight contour for his labyrinthine sets and corkscrew camera movements and looming or receding figures. The film opens with virtuoso tracking shots as the camera follows sinuously and patiently a car with a bomb in the trunk, and it closes with another extraordinary sequence of tracking shots as a figure near the camera clambers, at night, with a radio receiver, whose distorted sound we hear. And in between a melee of characters, textures, and violent incidents combine elaboration and momentum in a way that reveals the advantage of genre form to Welles. One detail looks like the seed of *Psycho,* 1960, the harassment of Janet Leigh in a run-down motel includes a prurient, mentally defective desk clerk called "The Night Man."

Although the film visually and in narrative pace (alternating between the oblique and the baroque) is absolutely that of Welles, the view of society in it is general in the period. For example, the two policemen, Charlton Heston and Orson Welles, are handled as a complementary and antagonistic pair. The Irish cop is corrupt, but many of the criminals that he has framed were guilty, we are given to understand, so that his zeal has an ironic justification. The Mexican, on the

The Lineup, Columbia Pictures Corp. *Left column,* a ship in San Francisco Bay (1), the pier (2), passengers disembarking (3). *Right column,* a startled passenger (4) sees his bag stolen and tossed in a cab (5). The view through the cab's windshield shows a truck pulling out (6); *left column,* which the driver cannot avoid hitting (7). The cab backs off (8), resumes speed (9), and is flagged by a policeman (10); *right column,* who is run down (11), but who shoots from the ground (12), hitting the driver (13). Final crash and first title (14).

other hand, the hero of the film, is a sophisticated and just man who finally destroys the evil in the system, though he lacks the Irishman's canny instinct for crime and his willingness to fight criminals at their own level. His virtue comes over as a touch of rigidity.

Title	Warlock
Year	1959
Company	Twentieth Century-Fox Film Corp.
Producer	Edward Dmytryk
Director	Edward Dmytryk
Screenplay	Robert Alan Aurthur
Source	Novel by Oakley Hall
Photography	Joe MacDonald
Editor	Jack W. Holmes
Music	Leigh Harline
Running time	121 minutes
Cast	
Richard Widmark	Gannon
Henry Fonda	Blaisdell
Anthony Quinn	Morgan
Dorothy Malone	Lily Dollar
Dolores Michaels	Jessie
Wallace Ford	Judge Holloway
Tom Drake	Abe McQuown
Richard Arlen	Bacon
De Forest Kelley	Curley
Regis Toomey	Skinner
Vaughn Taylor	Richardson
Don Beddoe	Dr. Wagner
Whit Bissell	Petrix
Bartlett Robinson	Slavin
J. Anthony Hughes	Shaw
Donald Barry	Calhoun
Frank Gorshin	Billy Gannon
Ian MacDonald	MacDonald
Stan Kember	Hutchinson
Paul Comi	Friendly
L. Q. Jones	Jiggs
Mickey Simpson	Fitzsimmons
Robert Osterloh	Professor
James Philbrook	Cade
David Garcia	Pony Benner
Robert Adler	Foss
Joel Ashley	Murch

Title	The Manchurian Candidate
Year	1962
Company	United Artists Corp.
Executive Producer	Howard W. Koch
Producers	George Axelrod and John Frankenheimer
Director	John Frankenheimer
Screenplay	George Axelrod
Source	Novel by Richard Condon
Photography	Lionel Lindon
Editor	Ferris Webster
Music	David Amram
Running time	126 minutes
Cast	
Frank Sinatra	Bennett Marco
Laurence Harvey	Raymond Shaw
Janet Leigh	Rosie
Angela Lansbury	Raymond's mother
Henry Silva	Chunjin
James Gregory	Senator John Iselin
Leslie Parrish	Jocie Jordan
John McGiver	Senator Thomas Jordan
Khigh Dhiegh	Yen Lo
James Edwards	Corporal Melvin
Douglas Henderson	Colonel
Albert Paulsen	Zilkov
Barry Kelley	Secretary of Defense
Lloyd Corrigan	Holborn Gaines
Madame Spivy	Berezovo

The Manchurian Candidate, as often happens with films adapted from long novels, is both ornate and compressed. All its points are made hyperbolically, as punchy as the climax-ridden television programs from which the director came. Examples of its maximized handling of events are: a room-wrecking, table-splitting karate fight; and a winner of the Congressional Medal of Honor, surrounded by generals, media equipment, and happy crowds, describing himself as feeling like "Captain Idiot in *Astounding Science Comics.*" And this is in fact an apt comment on the plot of the film, which is basically a revival of the old-time Yellow Peril. This theme revived with the emergence of China as a world power, and it is here embedded brilliantly in a spate of pessimistic, topical subjects that include Fascism in high places, Congressional committees, momism, brainwashing, and finally matricide and the shooting of a Presidential candidate in Madison Square Garden.

The plot is an anthology of dark and topical American themes which wind like a maze around the suspicious investigating hero, Frank Sinatra. Sinatra, with the kind of detail that is typical of this film, bases his investigation on a recurring nightmare. A celebrated sequence is the brainwashing episode in which fact and falsehood alternate in slow pans of the camera. In these scenes continuous takes provide the kind of contrasts that would have been achieved by cutting in films earlier than the 40s, or in films later than 1962 when this film was made.

Johnny Cool, United Artists Corp. *Left column,* rooftop with Johnny Cool (1), who boards a scaffold (2), descends on the only unguarded approach (3, 4; *right column,* 5), to the gangster's executive suite (6), for execution (7, 8).

Title	Johnny Cool
Year	1963
Company	United Artists Corp.
Producer	William Asher
Director	William Asher
Screenplay	Joseph Landon
Source	Novel by John McPartland, *The Kingdom of Johnny Cool*
Photography	Sam Levitt
Editors	Otto Ludwig
Music	Billy May
Running time	103 minutes
Cast	
Henry Silva	Johnny Cool
Elizabeth Montgomery	Dare Guiness
Richard Anderson	Correspondent
Jim Backus	Louis Murphy
Joey Bishop	Used car salesman
Brad Dexter	Lennart Crandall
Wanda Hendrix	Miss Connolly
Hank Henry	Bus driver
Marc Lawrence	Johnny Colini
John McGiver	Oby Hinds
Gregory Morton	Jerry March
Mort Sahl	Ben Morro
Telly Savalas	Mr. Santangelo
John Staley	Suzy
Sammy Davis, Jr.	Educated
Katherine Bard	Mrs. Crandall
Elisha Cook, Jr.	Undertaker

Henry Silva plays the killer from Italy, and, as in Siegel's *The Killers,* 1964, we as spectators accompany the killer on his tasks. After a song behind the credits about Johnny Cool, a kind of updated "Mack the Knife," the film traces the hero's career from a child fighting the Nazis, to Sicilian Robin Hood, to adoption by an exiled Mafia chief who says, "I will teach you America." From then on America is defined by Johnny's cool acts of violence which first arouse and then disgust a restless divorcee. As Johnny Cool says, "I'm the one to do the killing. All over the country. They'll think they've been hit by an army." With an episodic form derived from TV the film follows Cool's cross-country route of unperturbed assassination. *Johnny Cool* is a harsh movie that anticipates later so-called exploitation movies, both in its unrelenting violence and in its sub-theme of the sexuality of violence; see for instance *The Wild Angels,* 1966.

Title	The Killers
Year	1964
Company	Universal Pictures
Producer	Don Siegel
Director	Don Siegel
Screenplay	Gene L. Coon
Source	Short story by Ernest Hemingway
Photography	Richard L. Rawlings
Editor	Richard Belding
Music	Johnny Williams
Running time	95 minutes
Cast	
Lee Marvin	Charlie
Angie Dickinson	Sheila Farr
John Cassavetes	Johnny North
Ronald Reagan	Browning
Clu Gulager	Lee
Claude Akins	Earl Sylvester
Norman Fell	Mickey
Virginia Christine	Miss Watson
Don Haggerty	Mail truckdriver
Robert Phillips	George
Kathleen O'Malley	Receptionist
Ted Jacques	Gym assistant
Jimmy Joyce	Salesman

The film was made for television, but it was found not to be family fare and so was shifted to the big screen. The early film was told in flashbacks as narrated to an insurance investigator. Here, developing an idea implicit in Siegel's *The Lineup,* the investigation is done by the killers, one of whom is concerned at the victim's lack of interest in survival. The foreground always belongs to the agents of death as they terrorize the four long flashbacks out of people who had known the dead man. The stress on professionalism in *The Killers* is an up-to-date aspect that has the authority of current convention to back it up in a way that the fatal woman theme, central to the earlier film, does not.